CHURCHES
OF THE
HOLY
LAND

Overleaf: *Jesus and Mary. Queen of Pilgrims. Church of the Dormition, Jerusalem.*

CHURCHES
OF THE
HOLY LAND

Gerard Bushell, O.F.M.

Photographs by Anna Riwkin-Brick

A SABRA BOOK
FUNK AND WAGNALLS
NEW YORK

CUM PERMISSU SUPERIORUM

Layout by Gerson Gera

CONTENTS

CHURCHES
OF THE
HOLY
LAND

THE HOLY LAND is entirely fascinating. Here are snow-capped mountains, hot, tropical valleys, rolling brown hills and clear, sparkling lakes, all forming the background to a world of personalities with distinctive racial, social and religious customs which is unique in the world. Above all, this Land is a place of fermentation for ideas, ideals and aspirations. Here, men and women have attempted, and achieved, superhuman things; they have changed their own lives and those of their neighbors, shaping the course of history far beyond the country's borders and leaving a legacy of the spirit which will last for all time.

To appreciate this Land you must first *see* it. For many, an actual visit must remain a dream; but there is a substitute, and a very good one, in our time. It is modern photography. The pictures you find in this book will help immensely in seeing features of the Holy Land as they really are. Obviously, only personal contact can make one experience the atmosphere of the Land; but you will be brought as close as possible to such an experience by a study of the illustrations. For nearly twenty years, I taught courses on the Bible and its associated disciplines without ever having visited the Land. Yet, a continual study of photos and maps helped me to understand and to explain accurately enough what had gone on there. A subsequent visit brings to life what one has seen before as if reflected in a mirror— and the visit itself is the more rewarding for the time spent in the preparation by pictures.

To understand this Land, you must *remember*. A long story lies behind almost every custom, institution and building you encounter here. There have been great gaps in the written story of it all, but many of these have been spanned in our own time by biblical scholars and others who have made the very stones of the Land speak to us of the things they witnessed down the centuries. So, side by side with the pictures, we have provided a word of explanation as to the precise history they recall: what people did here, what they thought, what they spoke, what they achieved and, above all, what they hoped for.

You will never appreciate the Land fully unless you *believe*—and pray, be it ever so little. This is not an ordinary country to be "done" by the tourist in two or three days. This is the *Holy* Land and, by the very definition of that term, we must stand in awe at the remarkable things that have happened and have been brought to pass here. It has been said that modern science is most highly developed in two spheres: nuclear physics and Palestinian archaeology. In the first field, the mysteries of material nature have been laid bare. In the second, superhuman achievements have been demonstrated to be realities. Yet, they remain, for the most part, mysteries. For a fuller understanding of them we must yearn in our hearts for an illumination on the part of that Power which so often intervened in human minds and hearts in this Land and largely shaped the human story through the ages.

The main monuments of these mysteries in the Land are in the form of art: synagogues, mosques and churches. For Christians, it is mainly the churches, with all the wealth of detail they enshrine, which capture our interest and invite us to remember, and to pray. Therefore, this book takes the form of an introduction to some churches of the Holy Land.

By its very nature, true Christian art cannot depict its subject literally, for it deals, to a great extent, with mysteries. Hence, its primary aim is to stimulate, to suggest, to evoke, to set inspiration free. In the Holy Land, so many religious themes have been treated in so many different ways through such a long period of time that, for the stranger, a word of explanation is often necessary. We must sympathize with the very architecture of a church—not to speak of the detail of its decoration and furnishing—before we can understand the message it transmits. The text of this book will help you respond, as exactly as possible, to the appeal of some great churches of the Holy Land.

The plan of the book is roughly geographical, moving from north to south. It introduces the reader to the churches in the north, down through the western half of the Holy Land. Then it begins again in the center (Samaria) and ends in the southern area, around Bethlehem. We have a precedent for this procedure in the Bible itself. St. Luke follows a similar design. His Gospel describes how Jesus of Nazareth had "gone round the whole of Judaea preaching, beginning in Galilee and ending here (Jerusalem)" (Luke 23:5). The Acts of the Apostles describes the converse course of the apostles, symbolized by St. Paul, witnessing to Jesus "in Jerusalem and throughout Judaea, in Samaria, yes, and to the ends of the earth" (Acts 1:8). Perhaps, after a study of the churches featured here, the reader will feel moved to proclaim anew the lasting ideals of the Holy Land: righteousness, truth, brotherhood and peace, wherever in the world he or she may dwell.

Prayer is the purpose of Holy Land churches.

NAZARETH

The Basilica of the Incarnation, Nazareth

THE NAME "NAZARETH" is a charming and significant one for Christians. Here, a young Jewish maid said "Yes" to God, and the long story of our religion began. Consequent to Mary's self-surrender, the Son of God entered our world personally in a particular place, time and family surroundings, took birth from a woman, took birth as a subject of the Law (Galatians 4:4). The great, modern basilica of Nazareth proclaims this mystery of the Incarnate Word, and it will be forever a source of inspiration to all who view or study it.

For many Christians, Nazareth evokes thoughts of "the hidden life" of Christ. In a particular sense, Nazareth itself is hidden in history. Nowhere is it mentioned in the Old Testament. Its name appears only sporadically in the ancient Christian records. In our own time, however, archaeology has bridged these gaps in recorded history and puts us in touch with our first forebears in the faith, the so-called Judaeo-Christians, the first converts to Christ in Galilee. That is why the new, dual church is of tremendous interest to all Christians everywhere.

Often, the Western tourist comes to a site like Nazareth, meditating perhaps on the mysteries commemorated, but inwardly asking, "Did it all really happen *here*?" Before all the evidence came to light, even a scholarly mind could locate the site of ancient Nazareth elsewhere. Today, especially since 1955, as a result of exact investigation conducted by Franciscans such as Fathers Bagatti and Testa, there is no further doubt that beneath modern Nazareth there lie the remains of human habitation, dating back to at least 900 B.C. And in those remains, the Herodian (Roman) period is quite clearly represented. In other words, there was truly a village here at the beginning of Gospel times, and it is quite possible that Mary's dwelling stood on the edge of the town, a limestone house which incorporated a cave for household use, according to the practice of the time.

The second question in the mind of the interested visitor is, "When did the place become a religious shrine?" The archaeologists have answered this also in striking fashion, and Nazareth is now known to be the site of one of the oldest places of Christian worship in the world.

Before 1955, there was a tradition that there had been a church here in early

Byzantine times, as far back as the sixth century after Christ. The scholars have uncovered and examined the remains of this very church, and now date it yet earlier, in the fifth century. Lifting the mosaics of the floor of this building, they expected to find only virgin rock or soil underneath. They were thrilled to find the floor actually resting on the remains of another building, which resembled in detail the synagogues of Galilee in the fourth century. This gave the clue to the nature of the shrine. It was a church-synagogue, built by a fairly affluent community of Judaeo-Christians, able to afford fine stonework and decoration and dedicated to commemorating the first mysteries of our faith, the Annunciation and Incarnation.

The most exciting finds, however, came in the form of symbols and inscriptions scratched on six successive coats of plaster or wash in a grotto, called the Grotto of Conon, next to the traditional site of the "House of Mary." From the nature of the symbolism and wording, it is evident that the shrine dates back to very early times, probably to the second century, A.D.

Finally, a most important piece of evidence has recently been found on the site of the new basilica itself. Inscriptions in the Aramaic language (that probably used by Christ and his first followers) give proof that texts from the Old Testament (Isaiah 55:1 and 13) were being applied, according to Judaeo-Christian interpretation, to the Saving Word to Christ, issuing like thirst-quenching water from sacred sources. There is obviously a reflection on Christ's divine origin and probably also on the Virgin maternity of Mary. Thus, on the site of Nazareth, in the last years of the first century, and certainly in the early years of the second, faith in the Incarnation and, most likely, in the Annunciation, too, was being spelled out on stone.

All this explains the importance of the lower church in the basilica: the whole is quite literally rooted in history. Visitors will soon be able to examine the actual constructions, symbols and texts which put us in touch with fellow-Christians of the first centuries, who venerated the Word made flesh *here*. In accord with the solemnity of the shrine, the austere dignity and impressiveness of the lower church derive from the form of the building itself and the skilful introduction of light. The walls remain simply dressed stone, and even the huge supports in steel and concrete are quite visible. Most impressive is the flood of light which descends from the cupola —down through a great star-shaped opening in the floor of the upper church— to shine on the exact spot where Mary's house must have stood, directly in front of the traditional sacred grotto. An altar is placed here. It is a plain table, devoid of decoration, and resembles altars found in the catacombs. The chief altar of this lower church is also correspondingly austere. The pillars which surround it and support the baldachino, and the three columns beneath the very altar itself, are actually made of unadorned, ancient stone shafts found on the site of the basilica.

In the great upper church we find similar restraint, imposed by the architect,

Giovanni Muzio of Milan. Outwardly, it is a great rectangular block, with two members projecting as façades. These two porticos show just what beauty can be achieved in masonry by engraving and relief on the surface, the graceful placing of windows and doors, variation in the color of materials and the tasteful display of statuary. The main (west) door is consecrated to the principal mystery commemorated, the Incarnation, and the theme of the whole façade is therefore Christological. It is surmounted by a bronze statue of Christ upon whose face there is an expression of solemnity, even of sadness. Yet, the book which rests on the left arm, and the position of the right hand—raised, with the three fingers pointing upwards before the face—represent a Christ who stops, questions, challenges, and prepares one for the graces available at this shrine.

Below this figure, in descending order, are statues of Mary and Gabriel, of the four evangelists, texts from the Old and New Testaments—all surrounding the great west window. Above the door is the inscription, *Verbum Carno Factum Est:* "The Word was made Flesh." The statue of Mary, with the face turned away in profile and a hand raised in puzzlement at the angel's strange announcement, is one of the artistic masterpieces of the whole basilica.

The other portico (south) is devoted to Mary. The façade is divided by criss-cross markings and carries the full text of the *Salve, Regina* ("Hail, Holy Queen") in Latin. A statue of Mary, a frank young maid in peasant's smock, is already in place above this door.

Inside, the atmosphere, created by the ingenious use of functional form and light, is that of a true church, a place for worship, a place for instruction. Here, there is no striving for effect. Ample free space, 1150 square meters of it, is provided for the prayerful worship of parishioners and pilgrims. A flood of sunshine comes down from the cupola which, inside, is decorated with prefabricated panels which give the impression of an immense flower covering the sanctuary. There will be three altars in the upper church which, by way of contrast with those of the lower area, will be highly decorated in marble.

Color is already appearing in the interior of the vast structure, particularly in the form of windows and mosaics. Windows in the lower church were fashioned in Austria, Lydia Roppolt being responsible for the designs, while the actual work was carried out in the Cistercian Abbey of Schlierbach. The window nearest the grotto is intended to introduce the visitor to the central mystery here, and represents the Annunciation of the angel to Mary. The heavenly visitor is almost devoid of any human characteristics beyond face and arms, while Mary listens with hand to ear to his extraordinary communication. Other windows recall to us those praises of the Virgin so familiar to Western Catholics from the Litany of Loreto: Seat of Wisdom, Spiritual Vessel, Gate of Heaven, Mystical Rose—all portrayed in graphic symbols.

On the north side of the building, where the light is not so strong, clearer glass is used and the theme is that of Mary conceived as the "City on a mountain." Sixteen other windows near the entrance show her in glory, as the "Heavenly Jerusalem," adorned with all manner of precious stones. Two stairways lead up from the lower to the upper church and these are lit by six windows portraying Mary's many virtues, especially that of purity: open, transparent window, enclosed garden, mysterious spring, crown of twelve stars.

Musical magnificence will be part of the worship here, and therefore a special feature of the furnishing will be the organs, one of which is already in position in the lower church. Constructed by the firm of Tamburini in Crema, Italy, it was finally installed at Nazareth on January 27, 1967. It has two keyboards, each with sixty-one keys, and a pedal-board with thirty-two keys. The mechanism of the manuals and pipes consists of a delicate electro-pneumatic apparatus.

The bells of the basilica are also in position in their special campanile of discreet proportions on the southeast corner. They were cast by the Italian firm of Barigozzi, and solemnly consecrated in the Church of Sant' Angelo, Milan, by Cardinal Colombo in 1967. The seven bells were dedicated to Christ Crucified, The Immaculate Virgin, Christ Risen, St. Francis of Assisi, St. Joachim, St. Anne, and St. Justus.

Rich mosaic already adorns the floor of the upper church. The variously colored marbles celebrate the titles bestowed upon Mary by the Church universal, together with the coats of arms of the Popes who were especially responsible for their proclamation. The long "carpet" of mosaic from the church door to the center has the arms of Pope Paul VI at one end and that of Pope John XXIII at the other, an allusion to the fact that it was the latter who heartily approved the project of building the basilica on March 2, 1959.

The monument is crowned by the cupola, placed above the site of Mary's house and rising some forty meters above the floor of the upper church. Inside, it is decorated with panels, as stated, while outside, it is surmounted by a lantern which, like a great star, will constantly recall to the whole countryside the mysteries remembered in this place. In form, the cupola resembles, more than anything else, a great space-capsule come to rest on its broad base above the building. Perhaps there is unconscious symbolism here. In modern times, we are intent on exploring the realms of space and fascinated by the mysteries of the unseen. The Nazareth basilica reminds us that Someone once actually entered our world from "the heavens," took the substance of our humanity, shared the flesh of a Virgin Mother, and was made incarnate for us *here*.

Thus, the authentic memory of the Annunciation and Incarnation has been preserved by architecture through the centuries, and skilful explanations by our archaeologists supplement the ancient traditions of the Christian Church. Five religious monuments have stood here, almost from the time of the apostles onward: the church-synagogue, the Byzantine basilica, the Crusader basilica, the Franciscan church (hastily run up in 1730, expanded in 1870 and demolished in 1955), and, finally, the wonderful new structure, begun on October 3, 1960 and substantially completed in 1966. The work of decoration continues, and it will be completed only after many years, with artists and craftsmen from many lands making their contributions. In this way, the church will truly stand as a monument to the devotion of world-wide Christianity, and the final beauty of the basilica will be as universal and timeless as the faith which inspired it.

Greek Catholic Synagogue-Church

THE GREEK CATHOLIC CHURCH of the Melchite Rite stands in an alley running westward from the center of Nazareth. It is in a *souq* or market section, and here one gets a vivid picture of Arabic Nazareth, with its flowing robes, trilling music and appetizing, spicy smells.

The twin towers and central dome of the church, common in Eastern church architecture, are to be seen above the roof tops. There is an annex to the left of the main building, with the small notice reading "Synagogue." It marks the traditional site where Nazareth's place of Jewish worship stood in ancient times and where Jesus would have worshipped in his youth. The buildings were turned into a Christian shrine by the Franciscans in 1741 and handed over to the Greek Catholics in 1771.

The interior of the little building is quite plain, with a simple altar standing close to the east wall. The usual Greek-rite icon-stand or *iconostasis* is absent. During the Moslem occupation, the name *Madrassat el-Messiah* (Christ's School) perpetuated the belief that it was on this spot that Jesus studied as a child.

A sixth-century pilgrim from Italy, known as the Anonymus Placentinus, has left us with the impression that the town of Nazareth in his time was still largely Jewish. For Christian visitors, the synagogue was a major attraction, for they were shown the place in class occupied by Jesus while learning his alphabet. The bench used by him was supposed to be too heavy to be lifted except by Christian hands, and the Jewish folk of the time good-naturedly went along with the legend by making burlesque and predictably futile attempts to move it.

The grown-up Christ also functioned in the Nazareth synagogue as instructor of his fellow-worshippers. Evidently, his ideas were disturbing, for it was in the synagogue that he became estranged from his townsmen and finally abandoned Nazareth for a second home town, Capernaum.

16

An example of how Jesus taught when "called to the Torah" in the synagogue is found in the Gospels: "And he came to Nazareth, where he had been brought up; and he went to the synagogue, as his custom was, on the Sabbath day. And he stood up to read; and there was given to him the book of the prophet Isaiah. He opened the book and found the place where it was written, 'The Spirit of the Lord is upon me, because he has anointed me to preach good news to the poor. . .' All spoke well of him and wondered at the gracious words which proceeded out of his mouth; and they said, 'Is not this Joseph's son?'" (Luke 4:16–22).

Jesus' further address on this occasion soon produced a contrary impression on his hearers. "When they heard this, all in the synagogue were filled with wrath. And they rose up and put him out of the city, and led him to the brow of the hill on which their city was built, that they might throw him down headlong. But passing through the midst of them he went away" (Luke 4:28–30).

Greek Catholic Church, Nazareth.

The site of this attempt on Jesus' life has long been pointed out as the towering crag well outside the town limits of Nazareth (The Mount of the Precipice); but it is thought today that it would have been much closer to the synagogue, possibly the elevation overlooking the gully through which Nazareth's main road now passes on the way to Tiberias.

Mary's Well.
Greek Orthodox Church of the Annunciation

WESTERN CHRISTIANS USUALLY think of the announcement by the angel to Mary as having happened in Mary's home. An Eastern tradition places its beginning at a public spot, the town well from which Mary would have gone to draw water and, perhaps, gossip a little. This time the dialogue was different. God spoke to her through an angel. An apocryphal Infancy Gospel, known as *The Protoevangelium of James,* tells us: "And Mary took the pitcher and went out to draw water. And behold a voice said, 'Hail thou who art favored, the Lord is to be with thee, who art blessed amongst women.'"

Nowadays, the site of Mary's Well is shown a few hundred yards north of the center of Nazareth, at the side of the main highway. A semi-circular arch and wall protects the outlet, now in the form of pipes, though the womenfolk no longer come here bearing water-pots on their heads. Most of them simply turn a tap in the kitchen, the town being linked to the general water-supply system of the area.

Historically, the source of the water of Mary's Well lay further back, about 162 yards northwest. This was the original holy site, and a shrine was built close by, as soon as Christians were able to control such a public place, after the expulsion of Nazareth's Jews (in 630). This sanctuary, known as St. Gabriel's, now forms the crypt of the present Greek Orthodox church.

The upper church is, like so many other Eastern-rite buildings, square in shape and measures forty-eight feet on each side. The hand-carved icon-stand (*iconostasis*) and the pulpit must have taken years of patient, devout labor to fashion. The holy pictures are rich in oriental ornamentation and elaborate familiar themes. To the right, facing the altar, there is a representation of the glorified Christ, king and high priest; opposite is an image of Mary and Child, reminding Western Catholics of the icon venerated as "Our Lady of Perpetual Help." Other images are those of St. John the Baptist, St. George, and Sts. Constantine and Helena.

Going down several steps into the crypt of the Church, one finds a light beneath the altar, marking the traditional source of the spring which has flowed here for centuries. On the wall to the left is a well-top, with a small aluminum bucket on a rope for drawing the sweet water from below. Around the rim of the lid are traces of an almost obliterated Greek inscription reading, most likely, "Hail Mary, the Lord is with thee!" An Arabic notice proclaims, "Annunciation of the Virgin," and "well of water." A silver plaque recalls the Eastern tradition: the angel speaking to Mary beside the well.

The present church was begun in 1767. A change in the traditional location of Mary's house led to the story of the Annunciation being attached to this building. Hence, instead of being known as "Saint Gabriel's," the official title in Arabic is *Keniset el-Bishara,* "Church of the Annunciation." The Greek Orthodox faithful of Nazareth prefer the simple name, "Mary's House." Thus, the mystery of the Annunciation is venerated in quite different spots by Latins and Orthodox in Nazareth. The fact that it is still worshipped with equal devotion by all is, of course, of paramount importance, over and above all differences of tradition and location.

Tabor rises over the plain of Esdraelon.

MOUNT TABOR

Basilica of the Transfiguration

IN GALILEE, AT the eastern end of the green and gold valley of Esdraelon, the great peak of a mountain rises 1929 feet above the surrounding plain. Its name is Tabor.

On its crown, visible for miles around, is a cluster of buildings, having as their main glory the majestic Basilica of the Transfiguration which seems ready to sail right off the peak like some sleek, lofty vessel, its prow proudly pointed towards the east. Even from afar, we are reminded that the word "nave" means "ship." Within the building itself, we are struck by the skill of an architect who can seize on the essentials of a site, a situation and a mystery, express its meaning in stone, mosaic and bronze, and illumine it all through alabaster with the light of the sun itself. It is small wonder that many people think this basilica to be the finest church in the Holy Land.

Climbing the zig-zag road to the mountain top, you enter the plateau area through an archway known as Bab el-Hawa: "Gate of the Wind." Even in summer, there are cooling breezes here; but it is the enthralling view of a great area of Galilee and beyond that makes you realize that you are now truly close to the skies.

Tabor has impressed man's religious sense, far over and above its value as a citadel. In fact, warriors have seemed loath to contest its possession for very long. The great stone fortifications you see round the mountain top were hardly used by the Saracen builders at all (1212–18). Here, on the other hand, religiously minded people have dwelt intermittently from the Stone Age to the present, adoring the Lord of Creation—who seems so close—with sacrifice, prayer and song.

Long before the Hebrew people came, Canaanites here spilt the blood of animals in honor of their gods. Centuries later, the prophet Hosea had to chide his own folk for performing similar pagan rites (Hosea 5:1–7). From this mountain, Barak, under the inspiration of the prophetess Deborah, led down his troops in a most unstrategic move, but was granted the victory which gave the enchanting Valley of Esdraelon to the Hebrews and united their northern and central clans.

In Hebrew poetry, three famous mountains are lined up in praise of God: snow-capped Hermon in the north, Tabor itself, and the "little mountain," which is the most important of all in the psalmody, not really "Little Hermon," but Mount

Zion (Jerusalem) far to the south (Psalm 41 (42):7). Tabor, with Hermon, is constantly regarded as a special manifestation of God's glory on earth, where his very voice seems to be audible: "The north and the south, thou hast created them; Tabor and Hermon joyously praise thy name" (Psalm 89:12).

In Christian tradition, an event of great splendor and joy also occurred on a mountain: the mysterious transfiguration and wonderful change in Christ's personal appearance, linking him directly with the Law and the prophets, Moses and Elijah, and, as such, expressly approved by the voice of God: "And as he was praying, the appearance of his countenance was altered, and his raiment became dazzling white. And behold, two men talked with him, Moses and Elijah, who appeared in glory and spoke of his departure, which he was to accomplish at Jerusalem" (Luke 9:29–31).

Which was the mountain: one of the sacred three, Hermon, Tabor or Zion? Its name is nowhere written in the New Testament. Christian memory alone can decide, and it is certain that, very early, the great event was linked with Tabor. Already in 150, the apocryphal *Gospel According to the Hebrews* has it so, and by the year 350 the association is taken for granted. The modern basilica houses ancient architectural monuments to this long tradition.

Coming down the cypress-lined drive from Bab el-Hawa, one's attention is soon fixed on the façade of the basilica, seen through the iron gates of the enclosure. A curiously-worded notice on the left gate-post discourages any visitor who may feel an urge to leave his or her name for posterity on the church walls. A visit to the northern outside wall will explain the reason for this terse text: "If you believe in God, you are welcome to pray. . . . If you are vain and callous about the rights and property and feelings of others, write your name on our walls."

The basilica is Roman-Syrian in style, a type of architecture which flourished particularly in the fourth and fifth centuries. Built in 1921–1924, its cream stone is still comparatively fresh, but is now showing signs of exposure to the fog, wind and rain which sometimes envelop this mountain-top for days on end. The structure of the façade sets the main theme. It is triple, recalling the three great personages who appeared in the Transfiguration. Thus, the two towers house age-old shrines dedicated to Moses and Elijah, and are made distinctive by the entrance which is separated from the main building, forming a narthex or porch open to the sky. Oriental motifs in decoration and two alabaster windows in the towers introduce us to other features of which the architect, Antonio Barluzzi, showed himself a master.

The bronze doors are huge, weighing one and a half tons each. Just inside the left door is a marble plaque reminding us of the purpose of the church and the date of its consecration (June 1, 1924), and recalling that it was built with "money contributed especially from North America."

The interior of the church is a striking vision, a wonderful transfiguration of stone, marble and mosaic. The central nave gives a full view of the eastward dome-shaped apse. It has two levels, the upper commemorating the divine nature of Christ, the lower recalling different manifestations of his humanity. The great mosaic above shows the three disciples awestruck at the sight of Jesus in ecstasy, accompanied by Moses and Elijah. We are reminded of a central truth borne out by Christ in his teaching: "Think not that I have come to abolish the law and the prophets; I have not come to abolish them but to fulfill them" (Matthew 5:17). The face of Christ in the design is lifted as if in converse with the Father and is full of gentleness and peace. The natural light of the sun illumines all. Only if you view it on a winter's morning at about six, when the sun first comes over the hills from Syria and glows softly through the mosaic, will you appreciate this central master-piece of Tabor. The memory of the artist who shaped it all, Antonio Villani, will always be held in reverence here.

Twelve steps lead down to the lower altar. Above it, peacocks form the symbol-ism of the main window, recalling the immortality which Christ guarantees. (If you press a tail-feather of a peacock in a book, it will outlast the pages them-selves.) This is a common emblem in Eastern Christian art. The lower sanctuary preserves centuries-old Christian monuments to the mystery in the form of low walls surrounding the altar. Those further out are from the time of the Crusaders, while those immediately around the altar represent the apse of the fourth-century basilica. So, as we pray here, we are in communion with thousands of fellow-worshippers of the glorious Christ through the ages, many of them, no doubt, now possessed of eternal blessedness themselves. The murals around the lower altar remind us of other "epiphanies" or manifestations of Christ's human nature: in his Nativity, in the Eucharist, in his Death, in his Resurrection.

Two small trapdoors on the floor can be opened to reveal the white stone which is the actual bedrock of Tabor's peak. If you are fortunate, the friendly Franciscan Brother will lead you further beneath the floor of the basilica and show you the remains of Canaanite places of worship thousands of years old, now laid bare by archaeologists.

The soaring height of the basilica's interior serves to raise eye and mind and heart towards the heavenly realm of the Transfiguration. Over a mosaic band is spaced a series of small columns. These ingeniously carry the great roof-beams, the wood having been especially imported from Czechoslovakia. The arcades graciously dividing the building into three naves are decorated with Roman-Syrian symbols, often found also in the ancient synagogues of Galilee. The five-fold cross of the Custody of the Holy Land appears frequently.

In each side nave, a stairway leads up to an altar above. That on the left is consecrated to the Blessed Sacrament, while that on the right is dedicated to St.

Worship of the Risen Christ (center), lower sanctuary, Tabor.

ET TRANSFIGVRATVS EST ANTE EOS

Francis, whose sons reclaimed Tabor for Christian worship through the favor of a benevolent emir, Fakhr-ed-Din, in 1531.

If you are energetic enough, you will be rewarded by a walk down a steep slope around the outside eastward apse. Here you will see how the architect's genius overcame the great difficulties of the natural terrain by lifting the basilica sheer off the mountain edge with great stone blocks, then refining the whole with delicate, dual, superimposed columns and windows of alabaster. In this part of the mountain, too, you will see the remains of hermits' caves and traces of defensive walls built by the Jewish general and governor of Galilee, later to become known as the historian Josephus Flavius.

The remains of the massive walls you see all around the plateau of Tabor were built in 1211-1212 by Sultan Malik al'Adil, but were dismantled in 1217-1218. The main Christian ruins near the basilica are those of the Benedictine monastery, destroyed by the above-named Sultan in 1212. You can still make out the main parts of the structure: the chapel, the refectory and the common room. Remains of the much older, fourth-century basilica are to be seen in the mosaic floor of the Elijah chapel (south tower), and also in another mosaic now halfway down the southern side of the exterior of the modern basilica, probably the floor of a baptistry.

The northern half of the plateau of Tabor belongs to the Greek Orthodox Church. The church of St. Elijah, with a small residence, stands on the site of an ancient church known to the chroniclers of the Crusades. Less favored for purposes of defense, this establishment was destroyed, with all its inhabitants, in 1183 by Saladin, while the Benedictines further east were able to hold out.

A view of the present Greek church as one descends Tabor recalls the conversation about Elijah recorded in the Gospels: "And as they were coming down the mountain, Jesus commanded them, 'Tell no one the vision, until the Son of man is raised from the dead.' And the disciples asked him, 'Then why do the scribes say that first Elijah must come?' He replied, 'Elijah does come, and he is to restore all things; but I tell you that Elijah has already come, and they did not know him, but did to him whatever they pleased'" (Matthew 17:9–12).

Cana

EIGHT KILOMETERS OUT of Nazareth, on the winding, falling road to Tiberias, there is a small, unpretentious town of some eighteen hundred souls, adorned only with cactus, olive and pomegranate trees. Its name is Cana.

Until fairly recently, the perennial, everyday problem here was water, and the

Christ transfigured, main mosaic, Tabor.

women of the town were to be seen carrying stone jars on their heads to and from the common well.

In the Gospel story, water is forever associated with Cana—water transformed. As the poet Crashaw has it, it was here that, "The unconscious waters saw their God and blushed." The young teacher, Jesus, was newly come from his experience in the Jordan waters where he had been baptized by John. He had but recently recruited some personal followers, most of them from the lakeside near Capernaum where they were fishermen. Invited to a wedding festival at Cana, Jesus showed himself more than an attractive leader. He changed the water of six jars into very fine wine, and the significance of this first indication of Jesus' true identity is largely elaborated in early Christian tradition, as the Fourth Gospel shows (John 2).

Today, three churches commemorate the mysterious episode in Cana. The modern Latin church was blessed and opened in 1905, but generations of pilgrims have worshipped at this spot, which our modern archaeologists have shown to be authentic. If you study the Visitors' Book, you will see the signature of a young bishop's secretary who wrote the name "Roncalli." Perhaps the charm of Cana contributed a little to the formation of that full, generous and sympathetic spirit to be known later as Pope John XXIII.

Father Egidius Geissler, a Franciscan, was responsible for the construction of the Latin church. He was a native of Salzburg, Austria, and his architectural plan is a minute but exact copy of the cathedral of that city. In the actual surroundings, the twin towers could symbolize the two partners of married life, while the red dome could remind us of their union in the bonds of mutual love.

The portico is of interest in that the bases, columns and capitals once formed part of a much older church which, as we shall see, had its own long history behind it. The church entrance has the invitation, "Let us enter the place where the Lord's feet stood." The interior of the upper church is wholly inspired by the theme of marriage. The picture to the left shows the first married couple of the Bible—Adam and Eve—with the blessing and encouragement, "Be fruitful and multiply, and fill the earth" (Genesis 1:28). In the center, the Gospel story of the marriage feast of Cana is depicted. Christ rejoices with the newly-married pair and bestows his approval while the whole company of simple village folk looks on, restrained and peaceful. Two other spouses, well-known in the biblical record, are also shown, Tobiah and Sara, reminding us of the lasting ideal of marriage as exemplified in their prayer (Tobit 8:7–10). So, in this church the institution of marriage is shown in its true, eternal dimensions, a symbol and efficient sign of the closest union possible: that of Christ with his Church, that of God with his People.

The lower church or crypt is a monument to the age-old veneration of the wedding feast blessed by Jesus through the intervention of his mother, Mary. A stone pitcher, copied from one in the Cologne Cathedral, reminds us of the

28

Cistern at Cana.

miracle. The picture over the altar shows the moment of Mary's intervention, with the six water jars about to be made famous.

Other elements in the crypt put us in touch with the countless Christians who have venerated the mystery here, some of whom have left us a record of their experiences. We can still see the remains of Byzantine sculpture: finely-worked bases for columns in marble, in their original position under the mosaic pavement. Four columns are to be seen in a row under the stonework of the present church. Of great interest is an inscription worked into the floor: "Honored be the memory of Joseph, son of Tanhum, son of John, and his sons who have had this altar built." It was long thought that the Joseph in question may have been Joseph, Count of Tiberias, who got permission from the Emperor Constantine to erect churches in the towns of Galilee in the fourth century. However, thanks to the work of modern scholars, it is now believed that the remains in the Cana crypt represent a building even older than that, and that it is actually a "church-synagogue" dating back to the third century, distinct from another place of worship used by the purely Jewish community (remains of which have been found)— proving that the miracle of the marriage feast was venerated here on this spot and linking us in spirit with some of the very early converts to Christ in Galilee.

The essential line of thought to be connected forever with Cana is indicated by the evangelist, St. John. For John and his followers at the end of the first century, the event was not just a wonder but the first "sign," and in the second chapter of his Gospel all the historical elements are made to yield their full symbolic value.

Espousals, marriage, wedding partners, bridal feast and life-long pledged love were all used in the Old Testament to express aspects of God's union with his people. So, also, the Christian era is to be *the* marriage feast, with Christ as the bridegroom of the Church. Though, at Cana, the actual time of Christ's glorification (redemptive Passion, Death and Resurrection) had not yet come, the submissive attitude of his mother and the servants caused him to anticipate history. Here, amidst the quiet rejoicing of the marriage feast, he gave the "new wine," inaugurated the New Covenant, "and manifested his glory; and his disciples believed in him" (John 2:11).

CHURCHES OF THE LAKESIDE

"THE LORD HAS created seven seas, but the Sea of Galilee is his delight." Thus, Jewish sages of old praised the charm of Kinneret, the harp-shaped lake which has no real peer in all the world. Situated some seven hundred feet below sea level, its climate is as warm as that of the tropical isles. Sheltered by surrounding hills, its surface is often pale blue and without a ripple. At sunset, it reflects the pink-hued mountains of the eastern shore. At night, it is illumined by the lights of Tiberias, or by the sheen of the moon shimmering on its gentle swell.

Most of Jesus' public life centered on the lakeshore, a place lush with vegetation, closely peopled by a sturdy race of fishermen, farmers and merchants, their outlook broadened through contact with the traffic on the famous *Via Maris,* the Highway by the Sea, running through from Syria nearby, across Palestine, down to Egypt. Like many teachers in the Bible (notably St. Paul), Jesus chose a crossroads of antiquity for the spreading of his message. Because he referred constantly to concrete realities, to life as it was to be lived, his words are full of pictures of daily lakeside chores: sowing, reaping, threshing, fishing, trading, cooking, sweeping, patching. So, provisions for life and care therewith was a major theme in much of his teaching. Here, on the lakeshore, he spoke of God as the supreme provider. Here, he showed himself the true Son of this Lord by supplying food for both body and spirit.

Church of the Multiplication of Bread

ONE OF THE most attractive wonders of the Gospels is that of the Multiplication of Loaves and Fishes, the feeding of a multitude from the most meager of resources. Exactly where this happened, we do not know. What is certain is that Christian tradition places the miracle at a particularly charming lakeside spot, and here churches were built to its memory.

The place was known in Greek as *Heptapegon,* "Seven Wells," in time shortened

The Sea of Galilee and eucalyptus grove, Capernaum.

simply to Tabgha. The springs are unique in their number and strength, as also in the quality of water they produce. Of old, Tabgha was the industrial suburb of Capernaum, for mills could be driven by the gushing streams. Potteries and tanneries were also here. The water, radioactive and warm, provided a spa for the local district. It served to produce lush vegetation all around, and in the Lake into which it finally flowed, fish gathered in greater numbers than anywhere else. The delta of Tabgha was a favorite spot of Jesus', together with its surrounding plain and hills. It witnessed some of the most striking of all the Gospel scenes.

The place of the Multiplication of Bread was located close by, as the fifth-century pilgrim Aetheria reports. About 350, a small chapel was fashioned and some mosaics belonging to this structure can still be seen. They lie beneath the floor of its magnificent successor, a basilica built between 400 and 450. In 1888, the German Palestine Society acquired the site, and in 1932 archaeological excavations revealed much of the remains. The floor plan of a large church came to light, fifty-five yards long and nearly twenty-two yards wide. The Benedictines, under the Abbot of Mount Zion, took over in 1939 and erected a simple church which serves to cover the ancient floor. Perhaps, in time, a more substantial structure will be built here, in keeping with the present monastery buildings which flank the church on both sides.

Under the high altar, in the middle of the church apse, there is a stone which, in the time of Aetheria, was believed to be the one on which Jesus placed the five loaves and two fishes (Matthew 18:13–21). Behind the altar, in the curve of the apse, is the wonderfully clear design of a basket containing four loaves, each signed with a cross, with two lake fishes at each side. An inscription in Greek, for which Patriarch Martyrios (478–486) may have been responsible, commemorates the mystery.

The most remarkable feature of the church's decoration is in the floor of the body of the building. For many years, this whole area was covered with soil and overgrown with thickets and actually provided a hide-out for local bandits. One can still see the scorch-marks of campfires. However, the full splendor of the mosaics is now revealed, and we can understand why people of old admired this as the most beautifully adorned church in all the Holy Land.

The floor of the central nave and the sacristies were done in a geometrical design, without any attempt at real artistry. In contrast, the side naves were richly ornamented, the motif being birds, snakes and plants observed in the small lake north of Kinneret, called Huleh. When this lake was drained by the Israelis to form a rich garden land, a small part was left as a sanctuary for birds and other animals.

In the mosaics of Tabgha there are plump geese and squat ducklings, herons, doves and cormorants, solemn storks and cranes. At the foot of the main panel

on the left (north) side, two peacocks face each other. Lotus and oleander, which still grow wild by the shore, are featured amongst the floral designs.

So, Christian art excelled here in a striking memorial to a great Gospel wonder which has in itself high symbolic value. As we shall see, it was at nearby Capernaum that Jesus' discourse explaining the deeper meaning was placed by the author of the Fourth Gospel.

Church of the Primacy

PROVIDING AND FEEDING is the theme of another event in the life of Christ localized at Tabgha: the commissioning of Peter to be the shepherd of Christ's flock after Jesus himself had gone: "Feed my lambs . . . feed my sheep" (John 21 :15–17).

Today, on a small plateau, a hundred and ninety-five yards north of the Church of the Multiplication, is a little black basalt church commemorating the breakfast scene which followed a wonderful catch of fish in the warm waters near Tabgha. The stone steps on which Jesus must have stood are mentioned by Aetheria as being venerated for the mark of his footprints. A Byzantine church was built here, and during the Crusades two churches stood close by, one dedicated to St. Michael and the other to St. Nicholas. In the mid 1500's, the memory of Peter's appointment was attached to another building on the site, a barrel-shaped vault such as is used as a workshop in many an Eastern bazaar. In the eighteenth century, the Franciscans gained possession of this building and added a façade and small apse at the back. In 1933, they rebuilt the church on the water-washed rocks, dedicating it anew to the memory of St. Peter.

When Pope John XXIII first convoked Vatican Council II, the idea of re-modelling this sanctuary was discussed, but nothing definite was decided. In January 1964, Pope Paul VI visited the spot, entered the church and knelt on the rock where, it is said, Jesus designated Peter as the shepherd of his flock. This marked "one of the highlights" of his whole pilgrimage, according to a member of his entourage. As he left, the Pope walked down the stone steps and bathed his hand in the waters of the Lake. There was no time for another ceremony he had been scheduled to perform: the blessing of the foundation stone for a new church here. However, on December 12, 1964, in Rome, this blessing was given, and the building of a new church for St. Peter at Tabgha is now foreseen.

Some who know the present little chapel will be sorry to see it go. Set in a grove of eucalyptus trees, bathed by the wavelets of the Lake, with its interior quite plain except for the rock rising from the floor called *Mensa Christi,* it is a fitting memorial to the events commemorated, majestic in their consequences but so

Christ's Table, Church of the Primacy, Tabgha.   37

simple in their origins. *Mensa Christi,* Christ's Table, itself is a reminder of how Jesus himself prepared breakfast, offering warm bread and fish to his tired, shy disciples. From his role as cook he soon changed to that of shepherd and delegated his task to Peter. For this, the apostle qualified not by wealth, brains, power or diplomatic skill, but solely by profession of unreserved love for Christ. "Jesus said to Simon Peter, 'Simon, son of John, do you love me more than these?' He said to him, 'Yes, Lord; you know that I love you.' He said to him, 'Feed my lambs… feed my sheep" (John 21:15–16). Thus, the Christian movement which was to encircle the world first took form in Tabgha bay.

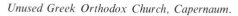

Unused Greek Orthodox Church, Capernaum.

Steps down to water, Church of the Primacy, Tabgha.

Church of the Beatitudes, Capernaum

THE CENTRAL PROGRAM of Christ's preaching is set out in three chapters of the Gospel and is known to us as the Sermon on the Mount (Matthew 5–7). Here are the basic themes of the message which Christ, another Moses and great prophet, derived from the past, and which he distilled and perfected and often preached from a "mountain top." Here is the fundamental teaching about God, our Father and universal Provider, about our brotherhood with all men, about interior motivation, about true spiritual life, about the need to choose the right road, putting into practice a sublimation of all that is best in Old Testament morality. But, none of it is presented in such abstract terms, for it was delivered against the background of the Lake with all its daily coming and going.

Most remarkable is the opening of the Sermon, a close summary of what God's rule on earth means for Christians. Each of the "Beatitudes" describes, in its first part, what true members of the kingdom are like and, in the second, tells us something of the kingdom itself. Like the preface to the Book of Psalms (Psalm 1), its keynote is joy, the "good luck" of those who willingly choose for God. This light-heartedness is the theme of all the Beatitudes: "Blessed are the poor in spirit, for theirs is the kingdom of heaven. . . . Blessed are the meek, they shall inherit the earth" (Matthew 5:3, 5).

Just across the road, northwest of the gate of the Primacy Sanctuary at Tabgha, there is a small, abrupt rise covered with dressed stones. The casual visitor will miss this altogether, yet it is probably the place where Jesus often spoke on things contained in the Sermon on the Mount. It overlooks his favorite spot, the Tabgha delta. It was an apt setting for public speaking, the terrain acting as a natural amphitheater and sounding board where the voice carries far and clearly. From here there was a view of lakeside life in all its diversity. Looking slightly to the right, the audience could see a city—modern Safed—on a hill so prominent that it could never be hidden.

The Franciscans got possession of this site, and in 1935 Father Bagatti made excavations there. He brought to light a little church with a single nave, decorated with mosaics, built towards the end of the fourth century. Adjoining buildings are probably those of a monastery. All this points to the hill *(specula)* mentioned by Aetheria as the traditional place of much of Christ's preaching, a fitting stage for a sermon on a mount.

Nowadays, the memory of the Sermon is preserved not at the lakeside but about a mile further westward up the mountain. Here, the architect of Tabor's basilica, Antonio Barluzzi, built another prayer in stone, the Church of the Beatitudes.

Church of the Beatitudes, Capernaum.   41

Commissioned by the National Association to Aid Italian Missionaries (the owners of the property), the architect has most happily achieved his double aim: to build a place of worship, and to preserve the impression of really standing on the Mount of Beatitudes. In memory of the eightfold sayings of Christ, the church is octagonal, built mainly of the black basalt stone native to the region mixed with imported materials. The walls support a copper-covered dome. All around the building proper there is a portico, to break the glare and to provide a fitting vantage-point for contemplation of the marvelous view.

Inside, the walls are simple, done in grey marble, but the interior of the dome glitters with gold mosaic against a background of blue. Over each of the windows is inscribed the text of a Beatitude. The mosaic floor is covered with symbols of various Christian virtues. The altar stands right in the middle of the church. Around the inner sanctuary there is an ambulatory encircling the whole area.

In its general lines, the church resembles others with a circular plan, for instance, that of San Vitale in Ravenna. However, the architect has shown his genius for expressing the mysteries of Christ, especially by the use of light. In buildings of this type, it is normal for the central features to be well lighted, while the side areas remain in semi-darkness. Here, we find the opposite. The walls of the ambulatory are each broken by a large picture-window at eye-level, offering an enchanting view of the sloping mountain, the waters of the lake, the surrounding hills and the blue sky over all.

The central feature of the sanctuary, the altar, is a work of dignity. It is made of solid marble and bears a prominent tabernacle, to serve also as a throne for Exposition. The whole is surmounted by a baldachino, supported by four delicately wrought columns. Marble and semi-precious stones from Carrara, such as onyx and lapis lazuli, form the background for other works of art. The panels of the baldachino have sculptures of the Crucifixion, the Resurrection, the Ascension of Christ, and representations of the Blessed Virgin, and Sts. Peter and Paul. A silver dove hangs from the apex, calling to mind the Holy Spirit.

Thus, we have a sanctuary worthy of the mystery it commemorates, the simplicity, dignity and joy of the Beatitudes themselves, "an architectural essay in atmosphere and symbolism." Nature and art are here combined to bring home the beauty of the original message. Stone, metal and mosaic form a lasting monument, but they blend with the background, the very one that Jesus knew. The mountains are the same as they were twenty centuries ago, covered in spring with flowers of the field. The birds of the air are still fed by the universal Provider. The Lake is as blue, its surface broken only by questing fishes. Here, more than anywhere else, we are drawn to ponder a central saying in the Sermon on the Mount: "But seek first his kingdom and his righteousness, and all these things shall be yours as well" (Matthew 6:33).

House-Church of St. Peter, Capernaum

THREE KILOMETERS NORTHEAST of Tabgha is the site of ancient Capernaum. This was the second home town of Jesus, the recruiting ground of most of his disciples and the center of the preaching of the Gospel. After Jerusalem, its name occurs most often in the written Gospels. The remains of only two buildings from antiquity still stand: the ruins of the synagogue (if not the actual one Jesus knew, then certainly one built later on the same spot), and the outline of a small basilica, standing on the place of Peter's home.

In the Gospel preaching, great stress is laid on *the house,* the one center in each town, known and open to all, not to be abandoned lightly by the preacher (Luke 10:5–8). While we know that Jesus entered many houses in Capernaum, it is most probable that his headquarters in the city was the house of Peter. The program followed by him on his first Sabbath there must have become regular: a visit to the synagogue and instruction there, then retirement to Simon and Andrew's house for the rest of the day, teaching, preaching, healing, so that "the whole city was gathered about the door." Finally, withdrawal from the house next dawn for prayer in solitude (Mark 1:21–35). On subsequent visits by Christ to Capernaum, it was always in the home of Peter that he received hospitality, so that St. Mark refers to it simply as *the house* without further explanation (2:1; 9:33).

The early Christians of the Capernaum area could not forget this house whose owner had been the chief shepherd of Christ's flock, and where so many wonderful things had happened in Gospel times. It soon became a place of veneration and worship. The Anonymous Pilgrim from Placentia tells us that, on his visit to Capernaum (570), "we repaired to the house of Peter which is now a basilica." A still earlier pilgrim, apparently Aetheria, refers to the house as being changed into a *church* within the area of the original walls. Thus, there was most likely a succession of shrines in this place, the first simple chapel being the work of Judaeo-Christians (who were comparatively numerous in Capernaum in the second century), while the more stylized structure dated from Byzantine times.

Archaeology has confirmed this. The Franciscan scholar, Father Gaudenzio Orfali, who was mainly responsible for the restoration of the synagogue, also brought to light (in 1921) an interesting octagon: a threefold series of concentric walls, each having eight sides. He was of the opinion that this was a baptistry attached to the Byzantine church of tradition; but further work, when the present Franciscan residence was built, showed that the octagon had an apse made of the same dressed stone. The whole is now identified by experts as the Byzantine church itself. That structure must have looked something like the modern church on the Mount of Beatitudes or the chapel of the Ascension on the Mount of Olives,

Jerusalem: twenty-two and a half meters in diameter, with a dome, an ambulatory inside, and a portico surrounding it. The main door faced westward, with two others in the sides.

The latest excavations of April-May, 1968, show that the Byzantine church was built over a house consisting of several rooms with stone flooring. About the beginning of the second century, some of these rooms were changed into a hall for assembly and prayer. Walls of this large chamber, found intact, bore inscriptions which Christian visitors scratched in the plaster during the second to the fourth centuries.

The decoration of the Byzantine building is most interesting and, in many ways, recalls the lavish adornment of the Church of the Multiplication of Bread. In the space between the outside and middle walls (which would have been the floor of the portico), the mosaic is very simple. The border is made up of edgings in black and white. The body is formed by concentric rings of large white cubes with a small black disc in the center. The geometrical exactness makes it pleasing to the eye.

On the floor of the middle octagon (the ambulatory within the church), only fragments of the original design remain. Floral motifs·predominate, flower stalks bearing red blooms of the lily family converge towards the center. In the northeast corner—with a bit of imagination—you can just make out the figure of a fowl or duck probably similar to those of the Tabgha church mosaic.

The floor of the central octagon (the sanctuary) is richly ornamented, suggesting an oriental carpet. The coloring must have been brilliant, with red, yellow and grey predominating. The edgings of the border are formed of geometrically placed cubes in four colors. The main body of the mosaic is made up of shell-shaped figures, in red, yellow and grey, each bearing in its center a little flower with grey petals. The overall effect is that of the many "eyes" to be seen in peacock feathers. This leads into the most remarkable motif of all: a great disk with rainbow borders surrounding a bird-figure in the center. There is no doubt that we have here the representation of a peacock, with tail fully spread, the common symbol of immortality. Unfortunately, the head and part of the tail design have been removed.

At the east end of the octagon, the lower courses of the apse have been restored and a simple altar slab erected. Liturgical celebrations are frequent. Thus is continued into our own time the Judaeo-Christian and Byzantine tradition, venerating on this spot the memory of Christ the missionary who made his headquarters here in the home of Simon Peter.

Mosaic from the Byzantine House-Church of St. Peter, Capernaum.

The Synagogue at Capernaum

THE MOST STRIKING monument on the grounds of the Franciscans at Capernaum is the partially restored synagogue of ancient times. This is a major attraction for both Jews and Christians, and hundreds of visitors view it yearly. Once a glistening white temple which dominated all Capernaum, it was destroyed by an earthquake and lay in absolute ruin for many centuries.

Father Gaudenzio Orfali, the Franciscan archaeologist, was responsible for its partial restoration. A tribute to him is written in black lettering on one of the four columns still standing, recording his achievement and also his tragic death.

In a scholarly report of the excavations (1905–1921), Father Gaudenzio argued vigorously that the building we now see is the one that was actually known to Jesus, having been donated to the city by a friendly Roman centurion (Luke 7:5). The majority of the experts, however, now hold that this is a different structure, built at the end of the second or the beginning of the third century. It is quite possible that under the present ruins lie those of an earlier, less ornate synagogue dating back to the time of Christ.

A study of the details of the ruins helps us reconstruct in the mind's eye the beauty and dignity of this building. Freely following Roman-Syrian styles, the architects fashioned a simple symmetrical structure whose massive strength could be overthrown only by a great convulsion of nature. The decoration of the building was most impressive, and some of the traditional Jewish symbols it utilized, still discernible despite deliberate destruction, are seen today on modern Israel's coins.

For Christians, the Capernaum synagogue will always be remembered as the scene of Christ's Eucharistic Discourse. In the Fourth Gospel, the symbolism of the wonder of the Multiplication of Loaves and Fishes is brought out by means of the sermon which follows it immediately (John 6). Written down at the end of the first century, it is really a reflection on the substance of Jesus' words, now understood against the background of the Christian liturgy. In fine, it is an explanation of what the Consecration in that liturgy means in the daily life of every believer. Christ is the living bread, giving us life here and on into eternity.

When Pope Paul VI visited the site on Sunday, January 5, 1964, he dwelt long in meditation on the Eucharistic mysteries. He recited the last verses of the *Pange lingua gloriosi* and, at the words *veneremur cernui* he bowed his head reverently.

When we, too, visit these lakeside spots, the wonder of the Multiplication and of the Eucharistic Discourse will be in our minds also. Here is a fitting place to read all of the sixth chapter of John and to renew something of Jesus' own Spirit within us, for "this he said in the synagogue as he taught at Capernaum" (John 6:59).

Ruins of the Synagogue, Capernaum.

ACRE

ONE OF THE most enchanting towns in all the Holy Land lies nine miles north of Haifa bay. A peninsula spreads out gracefully into the indigo waters, a semi-isle which seems ready to float off into the sea were it not weighed down by the domes, minarets and spires of its mosques and churches and, above all, by the enormous and ancient piles of masonry which were once its forts. Its name is Akko, better known to Christians by its more familiar title of "City of St. John of Acre," or Acre. With its natural port and strategic location, commanding entry into all north Palestine, it was coveted by every would-be conqueror of the country. It has a long history behind it, but the most interesting periods are those of the Crusaders and the Turks.

During the second hundred years of the Crusader occupation of Palestine (1191–1291), it was actually the capital of the Latin kingdom in the Levant, a second Jerusalem, the fate of the real Jerusalem being too uncertain for a seat of lasting domination. Thus, through this period, Acre was the headquarters of almost every section of the Latin community, especially of the Military, Hospitaller and Religious Orders. One of the latter, first set up in Acre, soon returned to the Holy Land to stay there for many centuries after the Crusaders had departed. It took over the finest ideals of the Cross-bearers and brought them to reality without the use of sword and arrow. This religious body continues its task to the present day—the Franciscan Order founded by St. Francis of Assisi in 1209.

One aspect of St. Francis' genius was his wish to share his spiritual good news with all men, irrespective of class, creed or color. He was the first to insert in a Rule for Religious a special chapter on "Those [Brothers] who go amongst the Saracens and others who do not believe"—for men whose spiritual horizon was not limited by monastery walls or even by the boundaries of their own native lands. (Incidentally, the word "Saracen" is not favorably received by many Easterners, having unsuitable overtones. I once knew an Arab confrere who insisted on reading this twelfth chapter of the Rule, "Those who go amongst the *Arabs* and others . . .").

On May 14, 1217, at a General Meeting of the new-born Order, St. Francis

personally intervened to set up the first "Overseas Province," in Syria. In 1219, he himself came to Palestine, visited Acre, possibly twice, and stayed on there through 1220, consolidating in this historic town the headquarters of his Custody (Guardianate) of the Holy Land. One still sees his brown-robed sons guarding all the main Latin shrines, officially on behalf of the Catholic Church but, practically, for the benefit of all Christians in the world.

In St. Francis' time, the Brothers of his Order in Acre had their house in a central position, quite near the *castellum* or main fortress. Eventually, however, they were expelled, many dying when, in 1291, an angry sultan, Melek el-Ashraf Khalil, wiped out the whole Christian community of the city. It was not before 1620 that the Franciscans were able to return to Acre and slowly make their presence felt there once again.

Church of St. John the Baptist in the Market

IN 1928, A new Latin church was built in a more central position in the town. The name of St. John the Baptist was transferred to it and, though it is frequently referred to nowadays as "St. Francis'," this title belongs, strictly speaking, to the residence and school surrounding it. The church is a humble little structure, such as St. Francis himself would have liked, especially as it is situated close to the people in the market area of Acre with the atmosphere of an Arab town permeating the narrow alleyways. So, if you walk around with the Franciscan pastor, you will hear him greeted cheerfully on all sides in Arabic, Hebrew, French, Italian and English—a sure sign that the spirit of St. Francis, the saint of the people, lives on in Acre still.

The church is built in a corner of one of the famous khans or caravansarais of Acre. This one, Khan el-Afranj (Inn of the Europeans), stands on the site of the Crusader Convent of Franciscan Nuns, called Poor Clares. It was these Sisters who, on the disastrous day of the overwhelming Moslem victory of 1291, cut off their noses so as to escape the attentions of the conquering warriors.

The church is Gothic in style, built of grey stone, with a small spire above an eight-sided base. Inside, the apse is vaulted, appearing triangular in shape. The worn inscription above the altar is being replaced by lettering in bronze on wood, reminding us that St. John the Baptist, the Precursor of the Lord, is the patron of the church. There are two side altars; that on the epistle side is dedicated to St. Anthony of Padua, the other to the Madonna and Child. Halfway down the gospel side wall is the picture of a Franciscan, Father Emmanuel Ruiz, a parish priest here who was martyred in Damascus in 1860 and beatified by Pope Pius XI

Church of St. John the Baptist in the Market, Acre.

51

in 1926. The picture at the end of the church is that of St. Francis blessing his native town, Assisi, shortly before death. Over the font is a small bust of Our Lady of Sorrows. The windows depict various Franciscan saints—with one exception, that of St. Aurelius, Bishop. He was the patron of Father Aurelio Marotta, the *Custos,* or Regional Superior, of the Holy Land when the little church was built. The premises adjoining are used as the parish residence and primary school.

Church of St. John the Baptist by the Sea

IN 1737, THE Franciscans built a modest little church quite close to the south sea wall. This was mainly for the convenience of "Catholic women" (as an old document has it), for Latins and Oriental Christians who had no place of worship of their own. The lower part of the structure dates from Crusader times and is located roughly on the site of the ancient church of St. Andrew. The name of the church is a reminder of what the historical title, St. John of Acre, really means. St. John the Baptist is the patron of the city, and this fact is commemorated by the little building which is to be found slightly southeast of the modern lighthouse. It was restored in 1947, but is now no longer used for public worship. The little tower lacks a cross and, within, the only religious emblem is a small plaster-cast of a dove on the ceiling, symbolizing the Holy Spirit. The premises were utilized for some time as a social center under the auspices of the Latin parish priest.

Site of St. John the Baptist's by the Sea, Acre.

Interior of St. John the Baptist's, Acre.

Greek Orthodox Church of St. George, Acre

BY FAR THE most popular of the saints venerated in the Eastern Church is St. George, the "Great Martyr" and "Captain of the Noble Army of Martyrs." In this matter of veneration of Christian heroes, the East is much more conservative than the West, where one holy person succeeds another in popular favor, giving us various "strata" of hagiography and veneration. The East, in fact, continues to represent the same holy persons, amongst whom St. George is always present. Devotion to him was especially strong around Acre and the present Greek Orthodox Church is dedicated to him.

This particular church is considered the oldest of all the churches in modern Acre, its foundations dating back certainly to the Middle Ages. It is situated slightly northeast of the lighthouse and is marked by a small red dome and cross. Inside, the building seems, at first sight, to be similar to many another, but there are characteristic differences.

In the iconostasis, the marble work is particularly fine, having been imported from Italy. Many of the icons or holy images are now nearly one hundred years old, bearing the date, 1871. On the right of the central entrance to the sanctuary is an image of Christ the Good Shepherd, with the familiar Gospel text in Greek: *Egō eimi ho poimēn ho kalos* ("I am the good shepherd"). On the opposite side of the entrance is the image of Mary and Child, like the icon known in the Western church as Our Lady of Perpetual Help. The third picture on this left side is that of St. George slaying the dragon. This is the most common representation of the saint, but it is not the earliest. At Bethlehem, for example, the saint appears without horse and dragon. Instead, he carries a spear and wears highly ornamented garments. Since this painting dates back to about 1130, some Crusader prince may have served as model. Nevertheless, the reverence of Byzantine faith shows in the face, which is serious, mortified, even sad with that holy melancholy characteristic of Byzantine art. On the altar screen at Acre there are the images of other favorite saints: Elijah, Catherine, Andrew, and such Eastern Fathers of the Church as Basil, Anthony and Cyril of Jerusalem.

Inside the sanctuary, the sacred books lie on the altar, covered with a cloth. They are in Russian, Greek, and Arabic. The kindly parish priest will also show you a simple silver chalice bearing the date 1781.

As is usual in Eastern churches, the woodwork is quite notable. Here in Acre, the pulpit is finely carved, while the bishop's throne is exceptional, showing on the back-rest a double-headed eagle. Around the pillars in the body of the square church are more icons, including St. John the Baptist and, again, St. George.

Greek Orthodox Church of St. George, Acre.

Shrines of St. George at El-Makr and Abu Sinan

IN THE ACRE area, there are other shrines which show how popular St. George was and how he was venerated by ordinary folk. At El-Makr, east of Acre, there are churches dedicated to Elijah and to St. Anthony the Great. Older still are the remains of a Byzantine church, known as St. Barbara's, whose fine mosaics show the figures of birds and animals. On the northern slope of the hill is a grotto dedicated to St. George, called *Mar Giries* in Arabic. The little building is almost circular in form: 7.30 meters east to west, and 8 meters in the other direction. At the east end, a small wall forms the iconostasis, almost hiding the apse. Five square holes for lamps form a cross in the masonry of the screen. The keystone of an arch, with a square cross, has been re-used. The ceiling is of natural stone, but on the west side there is a hole which gives passage from the grotto to the ground level above, and this opening has naturally captured the imagination of the people. The stories associated with it give an idea of the particular favors sought through the intercession of St. George. One concerns a woman who, at the end of the liturgical ceremonies, left the church but forgot her young child. Returning to look for it, she saw St. George carrying the little one out through the opening of the grotto. Special prayers were said to St. George for the granting of offspring and for the well-being of children in good health. On Saturday evenings, womenfolk still light candles in the grotto, for their own special intentions.

Abu Sinan lies close by el-Makr and also possesses a sanctuary of St. George, situated on the southern slope with an opening to the west. There was a natural grotto and in front of this a church was built, 4.60 meters long, 3 meters wide. A wall towards the eastern end served as an iconostasis, and the body of the building is divided by arches, north to south, resting on columns of various sizes and formed of ancient materials. Some elements are clearly Byzantine, so that the more recent church really continues a devotion which is centuries old. In the nave, close to the façade, is a baptistry carved from a rectangular block of stone.

Here at Abu Sinan, too, popular stories bear witness to the power of St. George. A Jew named Ben Jusef, despairing of being cured of a disease, once slept in the sanctuary. He was healed by St. George. Frequently, to obtain the blessing of offspring, the parents make a vow that the little one will be baptized in the shrine.

Thus, St. George, the powerful defender of the faithful, the great patron of England and of Russia, is worshipped also in many an Eastern village as the friend of homely folk. His tomb is shown at Lod (Lydda), the site of Israel's major airport, but devotion to him is strong especially in Acre. With St. John the Baptist's, his memory lives on, perpetuated in the Greek Orthodox Church and the shrines of the surrounding district.

Shrine of St. George, Abu Sinan.

CHRISTIAN
SHRINES
OF CARMEL

A GREAT MOUNTAIN range in Israel, running northwest from the Jordan to the sea, plunges abruptly into the western waters with a mountain known as Carmel. In many ways, Carmel is like Tabor, its second syllable being the secret of its world-wide appeal. Carmel is *Kerem El,* "The Vineyard of *God.*" Forming a natural barrier to caravans minded to pass down the coast, and almost impregnable from a military point of view, this mountain is nowhere noted in the Bible for a great martial or political happening. Only in the comparatively modern times of the Crusades was it fortified and guarded. On the other hand, it has had a lasting attraction for men of God: mystics, hermits, worshippers of the Lord of Nature, people who found the peace, solitude and sheer beauty of the mount unrivalled for contemplation. So it is that Carmel forms the climax in the description of loveliness found in the biblical Song of Solomon: "Your head crowns you like Carmel, and your flowing locks are like purple; a king is held captive in the tresses" (7:6).

Some of the most ancient inhabitants of Palestine lived here, and on this mountain sacrifice was often offered to a divinity who was known but imperfectly. Carmel was the scene of a crisis in the Hebrew religion, for it was here that the great decision was made (I Kings 18) for or against the one, true God. The aberration was personified by Queen Jezebel and her weak consort, Ahab, surrounded by prophetic bands. The champion of true belief was Elijah, whose name and achievement will be forever identified with Carmel by men who worship the same God still: Jews, Moslems and Christians. In Roman times, Carmel exerted its attraction even on Vespasian, Roman general and future emperor, who offered sacrifice for victory there. Suetonius, and especially Tacitus, seem to infer that the mountain itself was personified as divine: "The god Carmel has no temple but, in accord with the desires of old time (worshippers), it has an altar for those who adore" (*Hist.* II, 28).

The coming of Christianity brought a new generation of hermits to this mountain. The basic guide of their way of life was the spirituality of St. John the Baptist who, in his early days, possibly practiced the asceticism of a regular monastic life

Mary of Carmel with Child, High Altar, Stella Maris Basilica, Haifa.

59

such as that now known to us from Qumran. He was certainly commended by Jesus and the early Christian tradition of the Gospels as eminently worthy of imitation, a prophet—and something greater than a prophet (Matthew 7:9). So, he is described as the reincarnation, so to speak, of the greatest of the hermit-prophets, Elijah himself (Matthew 17:12). It was but natural that a constant Christian eremetical tradition should have centered on Carmel, and that the Christian ascetics there should have considered themselves spiritual sons of Elijah.

This tradition lives on still in the form of the Carmelite Order of the Latin Church, one of the most powerful mainstreams of mysticism in the Catholic world. The remote origins of the Order lie in the fact that Greek-speaking hermits from both East and West populated Carmel. The Westerners would have come from southern Italy (Calabria) and, after the Norman conquest of that region in the eleventh century, they would have been joined by many French-speaking comrades.

The coming of the Crusaders, with their sense of Latin organization and discipline, brought something new to Carmel. It is an ex-Crusader, Berthold of Limoges, who is credited with gathering the hermits who lived at the foot of Mt. Carmel into a stable community. His successor, St. Brocard, a Frenchman born in Jerusalem, framed the severe ascetic rule of the Order as laid down in 1209 by St. Albert of Vercelli, a Latin Patriarch of Jerusalem. This rule won the approval of Pope Honorius III in 1226, and was again confirmed by Pope Innocent IV in 1248. Thus, the venerable tradition of Carmel, refined and developed, soon spread to other centers of the Holy Land, to Syria, North Africa, Italy, Germany, England and later to almost every civilized country in the world, thanks especially to the powerful, ascetical and silent influence of the Carmelite nuns.

Church of the Valley of the Martyrs

ST. BROCARD MADE his first monastic foundation, not on the tip of Carmel, but in a *wadi* (gully) down the mountain, a mile and a half due south of the present basilica of Stella Maris. It is known to modern Israelis as Nahal Siyah (in Arabic, Wadi es-Siyah), or "Valley of the Hermits." From subsequent events in its history, it also acquired the name of "Valley of the Martyrs." To reach it, you must leave the main Haifa–Tel Aviv road in front of the modern cemeteries, work your way eastward around these and other restricted areas, and follow the narrow gully for a quarter of a mile. You first pass a concrete machine-shed and then, beyond, catch a first sight of the walls on the southern slope.

Excavations in 1958 and 1960 brought to light much of the original design of this ancient settlement, and a detailed study can be made in the museum housed

in Stella Maris monastery. The masonry, in its lower courses and in the stairways, shows fine stonework. To the west, one can make out the Superior's cell, so situated as to allow him to be the first to greet strangers. There is evidence of a large hall from which a flight of steps leads up to the chapel. This latter was built of a specially selected white stone which still retains its clear color. The shape of the church is rectangular, and there are three pilasters in each east-west wall to carry the roof. Most interesting is an arched entrance in the south wall, a spiral stairway of nine steps with the remains of a belfry above. The original church was built in 1209 and dedicated to the Virgin Mary. The building was enlarged in the second half of the thirteenth century when the adjoining monastery was put up. On this spot we stand at the cradle of the Carmelite Order, the place where St. Brocard's rule was first put into practice.

The Order's original coat of arms is a constant reminder of the beginnings here. The gully is finally blocked to the east by the sharply rising mountain side. The perspective of the two sloping sides of the valley with the hill beyond gives a shield-shaped design. This was subsequently elaborated to show three mountain tips, three stars, one each for Elijah (lower center), the Byzantine monks, and the Latin monks. Finally, there is a cross surmounting the whole, this element having been added by the great Spanish mystic, St. John of the Cross.

In 1291, with the fall of Acre, the monastery was sacked and all the monks massacred—hence the name, Valley of the Martyrs. From this time on, till 1631, Christian Carmel stood solitary by the sea.

Stella Maris Basilica

VISIBLE FROM NEARLY all the Haifa area is the great mass of buildings crowning the tip of Mount Carmel, 150 meters high: the Carmelite monastery and church called "Stella Maris" (Star of the Sea) in honor of the Virgin Mary. The buildings stand on a site where the divinity has been worshipped for thousands of years and where caves and grottos gave shelter to hermits and contemplatives. Together with the nearby convent of Sisters, this is the main Carmelite headquarters in the Holy Land.

A map made in 1235 shows the Crusader Castle of St. Margaret on Mount Carmel's tip and, close by, a church of St. Margaret staffed by Greek-speaking monks. It was on the ruins of this foundation that a new monastery and church were built some five hundred years later. The hero of the return to Carmel was Father Prospero of the Holy Spirit, born in Nalda, Spain, on June 17, 1583. After interminable bargaining with the Arab emir, he got leave, in 1627, to occupy a small hermitage still to be seen after five minutes' walk westward down around the

Carmel's story in the cupola of Stella Maris, Haifa.

Old Hostel on Carmel's peak. The shape of the natural caves is plain, but most have been stylized with walls and arches. The central feature is a small chapel built into a grotto and dedicated to St. Simon Stock, the English General of the Order who, in 1245, started the confraternity of the Scapular of our Lady of Mount Carmel, now known all over the world. Till 1762, Father Prospero's Hermitage was the center of Carmelite life once more.

In 1762, the Carmelites were expelled but, in 1767, they were back once again, this time with Turkish permission to occupy the ruins of the medieval Greek monastery, already mentioned, and to build a residence and church over a cave known as the Grotto of St. Elijah. The first stone was laid on November 15, 1767. In 1799, during Napoleon's siege of Acre, the monastery was opened as a general hospital and, amongst the patients, were some two thousand wounded French soldiers. After the defeat of the French, these men were ruthlessly slaughtered by the Turks and the whole site had to be abandoned. The last resting place of these soldiers is marked by a little pyramid just outside the basilica's main entrance—a sad reminder, too, of their former victories in Egypt.

Shortly after this, a Moslem notable, Abdullah Pasha, used materials from the ruins of the monastery to build himself a fine residence on the peak of the mountain. One can see traces of the Eastern style of architecture in this structure (especially in its arches), for it now forms the lower floor of the Carmelite Old Hostel, still the site of Stella Maris lighthouse.

In 1819, the Carmelites returned to repair their monastery and church, working under Brother John Baptist Casini, a confrere and skilled architect. After more interruptions, the first stone of the modern building was laid on June 1, 1827. From this time on till December 17, 1914, the Carmelites enjoyed comparative peace and were free to adorn their mountain top with monastery, basilica and gardens. During World War I, the community was dispersed once more and it was not until October 10, 1920 that the basilica and monastery were finally restored and, on that day, solemnly consecrated.

The general structure looks very much like a fortress—symbolic of the eternal truths, perhaps, but also of Carmelite yearning for security in view of the perilous past. It is rectangular in shape, 60 meters long by 32 wide. The basilica is in the center. It is Ionic in style, richly decorated with marble, mosaic, bronzes, statues and paintings. Beneath the main altar, below floor-level, is the grotto now known as that of St. Elijah. The Latin inscription above the entrance reads: "Elijah, the Thesbite, that great father and leader of prophets, once lived in this cave." The figures on the small altar inside are those of Elijah and the Madonna. Soot from innumerable votive candles, lit here through the centuries, covers the left wall and ceiling. This custom was officially approved by the Carmelite Superiors, as the little oval plaque above the entrance shows: "Let as many lights continually burn here as there are Provinces in the Order "(General Chapter 1931). Four bronze medallions in the floor in front of the grotto mark the tombs of heroes of the Carmelite tradition: Berthold, Brocard, Cyril of Constantinople, and Prospero.

The central feature of the whole basilica is the statue of the Virgin Mary of Mount Carmel with the Infant, seated above the main altar. Both hold the Carmelite Scapular, which has become the distinctive badge of the Order throughout the world. The statue has a long and interesting history. Commissioned by Brother John Baptist Casini, it was fashioned by a Genoese, John Baptist Caravanta, in 1820. Its journey to the Holy Land was interrupted by all manner of unforeseen happenings, so that it was seen successively in Malta, Constantinople, Toulouse, Marseilles, Gaeta and Rome. Many wonders occurred during its passage, especially multiple cures such as were not known again until the time of Lourdes. The statue was venerated by Pope Pius VII, kept in the General House of the Carmelites, Rome, and finally brought to its destination on Carmel twelve years after the journey began.

Six minor altars stand around the sides of the basilica, dedicated respectively to (clockwise): the Sacred Heart, St. Simon Stock (receiving the Scapular), St. Thérèse of Lisieux, St. John of the Cross, Sts. John and Theresa of Avila, St. Theresa of Avila. The windows of the basilica show many of these same Carmelite saints, while the eight large pictures below remind us of events in the life of Elijah and other prophets, as also in the history of the Order. All are the work of Brother Louis, a Discalced Carmelite. The large Latin inscriptions around the dome celebrate the glory of Carmel as spelled out in the Old Testament and applied mystically to the Virgin Mary. From the right: "The glory of Lebanon shall be given to it, the majesty of Carmel and Saron" (Isaiah 35:2). "Your head crowns you like Carmel, and your flowing locks are like purple; a king is held captive in the tresses. Ave Maria " (Song 7:5).

The floor of the basilica is done in black and white marble, fashioned to show a great star. Leaving the basilica, you see two long mural inscriptions in Latin, one, on the right, being a summary of the story of the basilica and its privileges, the other quoting a prayer of St. Simon Stock to Mary, "Flower of Carmel . . . Star of the Sea." Across the square outside is a column surmounted by a statue of the Virgin Mary, the gift of pilgrims from Chile, as the opening words (in Spanish) show: "Virgin of Carmel, Queen of Chile." Below, especially at night, one sees a magic panorama, that of Haifa and its bay, stimulating contemplation and prayer.

Elijah's Cave. School of the Prophets

At the foot of Carmel, near the junction of two main roads (Jaffa and Allenby), there is a tasteful little park called Gan Eliyahu Hannavi, "Garden of Elijah the Prophet." It contains places traditionally connected with the great hero of Carmel. One is a large cave which has been given regular shape, forming a room 14 meters by 8 in size, with annexes in the north wall. It is now a synagogue and a place of pilgrimage for many Israelis. The day I visited the place, a group of women were happily singing nearby, expressing the sense of joy which is a characteristic of Jewish devotion. The wall and ceiling of the east end of the cave are black with the soot, and warm with the heat of scores of votive candles which continually burn here.

The memories associated with the sanctuary by both Moslems and Christians are those of Elijah, Elisha, and their successors instructing their followers, the "Sons of the Prophets." Jewish tradition has localized here the spot where Elijah spent one night on his way to do battle for the true faith on Mt. Carmel. Christians also commemorated here the return of the Holy Family from Egypt, travelling up Palestine by the coast road before turning eastward to Nazareth. They are supposed to have tarried in this cave. Whatever the exact nature of their devotion, thousands of Christians and Jews have worshipped at this shrine, especially in Byzantine times.

Evidence of this fact has recently come to light when layers of plaster and wash in the cave were carefully examined by representatives of the Israel government. Numerous inscriptions, mostly in Greek, have been deciphered. They regularly start with the prayer "Remember," and contain names of visitors and sometimes of their families. About one hundred engravings found on the western and eastern walls represent, for the most part, Christian names common in the 5–6th centuries. However, others may refer to Jewish visitors. Proof that there were in fact Jewish visitors is found in the engraved figure of the *menora* (ceremonial candlestick), flanked by the *shofar* (horn-trumpet) and *lulab* (palm frond). Thus, the cave must have been a sanctuary holy to people of different faiths through the centuries, and therefore worthy of reverence, and a visit, today.

Chapel of the Angel, Church of the Holy Sepulcher, Jerusalem (See page 93).

Place of the Sacrifice. Hill of the Priests

OTHER SACRED SPOTS in the Haifa area are less easily accessible and more remotely linked with ancient Christian churches. However, thanks to Carmelite veneration, they do call to mind episodes in the life of the patriarch Elijah. The Arabic name for one of these perpetuates a tradition which is centuries old: *El Muhraqa,* "The Sacrifice." Seventeen miles by the mountain road southeast of Haifa, this site commemorates the central episode in the historic confrontation of Hebrew monotheism and Syrian paganism in which Elijah played the decisive role. The story of how the prophet's sacrifice was accepted, and that of the pagans rejected, is told in I Kings 18:21–39. The place was bought by the Carmelites in 1858, and a small chapel and residence were built. During these operations, evidence of a former foundation came to light. In 1911, the residence was enlarged and, for some time, served as a juniorate for young men preparing for admission to the Carmelite Order. The chapel contains a marble altar and a picture of the Immaculate Virgin, together with representations of the biblical story of the sacrifice. Situated 482 meters high, this site offers a striking view of much of the Holy Land: the Valley of Esdraelon, Nazareth's hills, Tabor, Kinneret, and the Mediterranean. Jerusalem itself would be in view but for the intervening mountains of Ebal and Garizim in Samaria.

On the eastern slope of Carmel, in the Kishon valley, there is an ancient mound called both *Tell el Kassis* ("Hill of the Priests") and *Tell el Katl* ("Hill of the Slaughter"). Here tradition places the final episode of the story of the sacrifice. With a forthrightness characteristic of the times and circumstances, Elijah pressed home his victory and had the rival prophets slain to a man (I Kings 18:40).

Thus, Carmel ranks with Tabor and Zion as one of the great mountain sanctuaries of antiquity. The special memories attached to it are still spread world-wide by the Carmelites of the Latin Church, men and women who, as both contemplatives and missionaries, carry the prophetic spirit into our own time. Flowering now once more, the Order will help many people choose rightly in the basic challenge of Carmel which is with us still: "If the Lord is God, follow him; but if Baal, then follow him" (I Kings 18:21).

Elijah routing the pagan priests. Hill of the Slaughter, East Carmel.

JAFFA

Church of St. Peter the Apostle

WALKING SOUTH ALONG Tel Aviv's main beach esplanade, one sees, right at the end, the profile of Old Jaffa by the sea. It looks something like a five-deck battleship of former times, the sturdy mast being really a bell-tower rising from the building below, the church and monastery of St. Peter the Apostle. The devotion of all Christians here focuses on the chief of Christ's disciples, for, in Jaffa and Lod (Lydda) nearby, the dignity and power of Peter were most strikingly displayed. Here he showed himself the rightful successor of Jesus by raising a dead person to life. Here he decided to exercise the power of the Christ-given keys on a large scale by opening up the riches of Judaeo-Christian faith to Gentiles by admitting them freely to baptism.

Jaffa today is a poor relic of a great past. It is now a suburb of Tel Aviv, offering items of passing interest only to the visitor: the charm of narrow lanes twisting through old Turkish walls, the spicy smells of Arab dishes, the strivings of artists and sculptors in modern studios, and the lovely view over sea and city from its hilltop. However, recorded history and archaeology have stressed the importance of Jaffa in the past. For centuries it was the chief port of entry into central Palestine. Many famous people came in here; others, like Jonah, went out. One fair lady of Greek mythology, Andromeda, was chained to the rocks at the harbor's entrance. (The street below my window is actually named in Hebrew *Mazal Betulah*—"The Maiden's Fate.") Only in 1965 did Jaffa yield its dignity as the key port of middle Israel.

During the Crusades, Jaffa was held fairly constantly as the main point of Christian contact with Jerusalem. Its hilltop was crowned with a citadel, St. Louis of France making it particularly strong by rebuilding the city walls with twenty-four towers. He also constructed a fine church with twelve altars and handed it over to the care of the Franciscans. From that time onward, they have been associated with Jaffa and the memories of St. Peter here.

Expelled with the last of the Crusaders, the Franciscans were back, at least temporarily, in 1520. In 1654, thanks to the friendly Emir Fakhr-ed-Din, they came to stay. Their main interest was in receiving pilgrims who entered the Holy

St. Peter's Church by the Sea and the old port, Jaffa.

Land through the harbor, and hospices, rather than churches, mark their story here. In 1830, a friary was built from material taken from the ruins around Caesarea. This became a hostel in 1890, and one can see it standing still between the sea and the modern monastery and church. These latter were erected between 1888 and 1894 on the site of Jaffa's ancient citadel. In the friary, two doors to the right (north side) of the entrance, there are two rooms which, though altered in Turkish times, still give some idea of the ancient fortifications with their circular shape, low ceiling and firing embrasures. The generosity of Spanish Catholics made the modern constructions possible, and all is still registered as Spanish property.

The church is richly ornamental in style, without being excessively baroque, though to modern taste it may seem a trifle overdone. Two Franciscan Brothers were responsible for the building and the decoration: Brother Seraphin of Palermo and Brother Bernardine of Rome. The church was solemnly blessed on May 24, 1891.

The façade in rose-colored brick is quite charming, especially in a land where grey stone and reinforced concrete are monotonously used in structural frames. The church front is decorated with the coat of arms of the Custody of the Holy Land and by smaller, metal designs: the five-fold cross of the Holy Land, the coat of arms of the Franciscans, and the tiara and keys of the papacy. The main window, best viewed from inside, represents St. Peter with the keys. The doors are huge, heavy, steel plates, designed to do exactly what they suggest: to keep people out. They bear the symbols of the papacy and the Custody, together with the Host and Chalice of the Eucharist, surmounted by the Crown of Spain. The secondary doors inside the porch are in proportion, but are of finely carved wood, as are the confessionals close by.

On entering the church, one is struck by the rich rose and red-grained imitation marble of the walls and apse. The brushwork is so fine that many think the material is genuine colored stone. The rear of the apse is in the form of two pilasters supporting a triangle (tympanum) and enshrines a large painting, by Zarlan, of St. Peter's main experience in Jaffa: the vision of Acts 10:9–23, whereby he was directed to make intimate contact with the "unclean"—that is, with the Gentiles as represented by Cornelius. Above the apse is a dove, surrounded by manifold rays, symbolizing the Holy Spirit who "fell on all those who heard the word" (Acts 10:44–47). A window in the rear of the apse illuminates the whole presentation.

Especially impressive are the six massive bronze candlesticks, together with the crucifix on the altar, the bases of which are decorated with the symbols of papal authority—the tiara and the keys—and those of the Franciscan Custody. Bronze plaques in the altar present scenes from the Gospel story of St. Peter. The main plaque, underneath, shows Christ giving over the keys of the church (Matthew 16:19). The one on the right (east) side presents the commissioning, "Feed my

lambs . . . feed my sheep" (John 21:15–17). That on the left shows the panic stricken disciples in the boat being buffeted by a storm which Christ soon calmed with a word (Matthew 8:23–27). Two small statues flank the main altar: on the right, St. Roch, protector against contagious diseases, which were then common in this part of the world; the other is of St. Francis, founder of the Franciscan Order. Marble is used in the altars, altar rails and floor, the latter being highly decorated with geometric patterns.

The most notable feature of the church is perhaps the pulpit, which is exquisitely carved in the shape of a living tree. In front, four panels, finely sculptured, show episodes in St. Peter's life: the miraculous catch of fish, the giving of the keys, the vision of Christ transfigured on Tabor, the washing of the feet at the Last Supper. Opposite the pulpit (west) is the first of the side altars, that dedicated to the Virgin Mary. A large drapery behind, and the imitation rough-wood finish in front, conceal the fact that, at year's end, this altar becomes a large Christmas Crib, to the delight of many children. The picture of Mary above the altar is actually an icon, a copy of the famous Virgin of Czenstochowa, Patroness of Poland. Its presence is a reminder that the Polish Catholics of the Jaffa area regularly worship here. The original picture was reputedly done by St. Luke, and its dark appearance resulted from futile attempts to burn it.

Other side altars are dedicated to saints usually venerated in Catholic churches, including St. Michael. The stained-glass windows in the body of the church were done by F. X. Zettler of Munich, and remind us of the Spanish origins of the present building. All the saintly personalities represented are Spaniards, with three exceptions, and even these have Spanish associations. Looking towards the rear of the church one sees three windows in the choir showing (center) St. Peter holding the keys; left (east), the apostle watching the vision of Acts 10; right (west), St. Peter raising Tabitha from the dead (Acts 9:36–43). On the ceiling, there is an inscription in Latin recording Christ's promise, "You are Peter, and on this rock I will build my church" (Matthew 16:18). Also on the ceiling, at intervals, are painted medallions representing the name of Jesus, the tiara and keys of the papacy, the name of Mary, the Custody of the Holy Land and, above the choir, a lyre with crossed trumpets.

Leaving the church through the monastery garden you will see a statue of St. Louis, King of France, who first established the Franciscans here in Jaffa, as also the two rooms containing the remains of ancient fortifications, as mentioned above.

The traditional place where St. Peter saw the Jaffa vision is quite close: you cross the square, Kikar Kedumim, walk south towards the lighthouse and descend the two flights of steps to the ancient level of the hillside. The room was once a small mosque, which is still marked by a low minaret, though no religious services

Statue of St. Louis, Franciscan Cloister, Jaffa.

of any kind are held here at present. St. Peter's great miracle at Jaffa, the raising to life of Tabitha, is commemorated in the courtyard of the Russian church of Jaffa where the girl's final resting place is shown. Once a year, there is a joyful festival in the grounds, with all the Orthodox faithful of the area taking part.

THE NEGEV

AT PRESENT, THERE are no public churches in Israel south of Jaffa. However, monuments to a vigorous and ancient Christian faith in this area are worthy of note and, if possible, of a visit. The extinction of the Jewish kingdoms in 722 and 587 B.C. left a vacuum in Palestine which people from the south gradually moved in to fill. This caused further migrations from Arabia and, among the peoples who, in the third century B.C., settled in the Negev (southland) were the Nabateans. Their special achievement was the watering of the arid soil by trapping the meager rainfall, guarding it like gold, and leading it on to cultivated areas by ingenious irrigation systems. Thus, they set up several garden cities in a land which is a veritable wilderness.

The Nabateans also engaged in trade, carrying luxuries from India and Arabia across the desert to such Mediterranean ports as Gaza. They were eventually conquered by the Romans, but their settlements came to life again with the coming of Christianity. In fact, the impulse given by the new faith, combined with a revival of traditional Nabatean skills, made the Byzantine period (4–7th centuries) the most prosperous in all the history of south Palestine. Amongst the most striking monuments to this happy time are the ruins of churches which have been discovered and carefully restored in many former Nabatean cities. Four sites are most interesting: Sobota (now Shivta). Nessana (Nitzana), Oboda (Avdat) and Kurnub (Mamshit). The last two are easily accessible from main roads.

St. Peter's vision of the "unclean," High Altar, Jaffa.

AVDAT

AVDAT IS 65 kilometers south of Beersheba, a yellow-brown hill of limestone in the very heart of the Negev wilderness. On the highway an occasional vehicle passes, but normally the desert silence is so deep that the wind itself can be heard. Caves, and stone houses in front of them, mark the face of the hillside nearest the road, but stairs lead up to fine masonry in the form of walls, bases and columns, ruins of the acropolis, or hilltop terrace, a public place occupied by all three peoples who successively lived here: the Nabateans, the Romans, and the Byzantine Christians.

Evidence of the devotion of the latter is seen in the baptistry and, above all, in two churches and a chapel which have been so well excavated and restored that one can still make out the details of their construction.

Christian faith dictated that the first sacrament, Baptism, should really crown a gradual initiation into a full share in common faith and worship, and so the baptistry was a building separate from the church. This custom was observed at Avdat, the baptistry being built on the terrace itself in the sixth century. It took the form of a room with three sides, with two columns standing at the entrance. The rear wall is rounded, like an apse, and in front of this is the font, in the form of a cross, rising above the surface, which is large enough for adult baptism. It was faced with marble slabs, one of them being found in its original position by the archaeologists. A smaller font for infants adjoins the main one. In a column to the left there is a niche, probably for keeping ritual objects used in the administration of the sacrament.

Close by is the church itself, built in the sixth century and known as the North Church. It is in the usual style of a basilica, with two rows of columns dividing the interior into naves. It had one apse, with a chair for the presiding bishop or priest, and on the walls are the marks left by the semicircular bench used by the other clergy. Traces of the altar have been found, and also the base of the pulpit, or ambo, used for preaching, which is situated to the left (south side) just outside the apse. The arch to the right was that of the vestry room *(diakonikon)* and here the remains of some ritual objects were found: crosses and lamps in bronze. (It is hoped that a museum will be built at Avdat where the movable items of interest which came to light will be displayed.)

To the southeast of this church is a similar, but more elaborate structure known as St. Theodore's, or the South Church. It has the customary three naves, a single apse, and two arches at the side. These mark (right) the sacristy and (left) the *prothesis,* or chapel where the Sacred Elements were reserved towards the end of the Liturgy. Evidence from charred beams shows that the roof was of cedar.

The marble table of the altar, though now fragmentary, has been reconstructed and set in its original position. Sufficient materials were also found to enable scholars to put together parts of the chancel-screen, marked with ornamented crosses and separating the sanctuary from the body of the church. On the walls there is evidence that they were once adorned with frescoes.

On this site were also found several inscriptions, which give an idea of the purpose of the church and the character of its congregation. An epitaph for the grave of a certain Zachary, son of John, says that he lies buried here "in the *martyrion* of St. Theodore." Another is for Zachary, son of Erasimus, who died in 581 and for whom a quasi-liturgical prayer is inscribed: "Lord, let his soul rest amongst thy saints. Amen." The epitaph for Germanus, son of Alexander, states that he died at the age of seventeen, regrettably "celibate," that is, without leaving sons or daughters. From these inscriptions it is clear that the church was in the care of a family of priests who have left behind some details of their lives. (The clergy at this time were, of course, married, as are many of the Greek rite today.) The altar table itself provides another inscription: "For Kassieus' and Victor's salvation."

In several grottos, wall carvings *(graffiti)* have been found, giving some idea of the way of life in Christian times at Avdat. The commercial interests of these folk are illustrated by special designs: men aboard a ship at full sail, ploughing through the sea; a rider on a horse at full gallop; camels fully loaded; animals fighting. Pictures of plants recall how these people continued to make the wilderness bloom through the skilful use of water. Other engravings are of a religious nature. One shows two male figures, each with a cross over the head. One holds the shaft of a long cross, another transfixes the head of a serpent on the ground. Most probably this is reference to Sts. George and Theodore, and to a devotion practiced by Christians of ancient Avdat.

Private buildings provide similar evidence. One room, now known as the Cave of the Crosses, has two crosses in relief surrounded by circles in the ceiling, a sculptured human figure, and the heads of animals. Another has a niche with crosses engraved on each side together with palm leaves—a fairly common Christian symbol of life. At the foot of the hill, close by the main road and the gasoline station, is an ancient bathhouse dating from Byzantine times. On one door-post, written in Greek, are the words, "Lord, grant help to Stephen."

Thus, at Avdat, Christians have an unusual link with fellow-worshippers of Byzantine times. The site, almost untouched by vandals and amateur explorers, yielded a rich treasure of the past. For the restoration, we are indebted especially to Professor Avi-Yonah, of the Hebrew University, Jerusalem, and to the generosity of Americans who made it all possible through the American Special Cultural Program for Israel.

KURNUB

FOUR KILOMETERS EAST of Dimona, in the Negev, lie the ruins of another city founded by the Nabateans: Kurnub (probably known in Byzantine times as Mampsis). A visit in the early morning brings home the desolation of a once thriving center of agriculture, trade, and military activity. The only sound one is likely to hear is the thin piping of a shepherd's flute from a Bedouin camp far away. During my visit, a small fox was the only sign of life amidst the golden masonry.

With a comparatively abundant supply of water assured by the skilful blocking of a valley, Kurnub was never abandoned as other Negev cities were when their cisterns finally ran dry. It is almost flat, in contrast to Avdat, and therefore had to be protected by a wall all around. This controlled the spread of the town. So, in the successive occupation by Nabateans, Romans, and Byzantine Christians, room for the growing population was improvised from existing buildings; the earlier lavish windows and doorways, for example, being sealed up to form new apartments. This is now of great assistance to our archaeologists as they try to reconstruct and date the various strata of the city.

Of interest to us here is the fact that two fine churches were built by Byzantine Christians, each having its own characteristics. The Eastern Church is in the form of a foyer or atrium (17 meters by 17), and the church proper (27 meters by 15). The architects were forced to comply with the existing conditions of a built-up area and could not carry out the usual elaborate church design fully. The entrance is in the form of a broad flight of steps leading to doors in the north wall of the atrium. Again, the church itself is not quite symmetrical, the apse and altar being a little off-center. In spite of this, the builders produced a fine basilica. In the atrium there was a cistern to catch and guard every drop of water that fell on the roof of the church and its adjoining buildings. The church proper has the usual three naves and a roof made of woodwork and tiles supported by two rows of nine columns with two half-columns in each row. Some bases and pediments are still to be seen, the two in the sanctuary showing the fine skill of the craftsmen responsible.

The apse housed the sanctuary, and we can still see the remains of the base of an altar which was carefully removed. A three-tiered seat for the clergy ran around the wall of the apse behind the altar. In front of the sanctuary, the base of the pulpit or ambo can be seen.

At each side of the sanctuary are the customary rooms, one being the sacristy

Avdat. Ruins of homes still marked with Christian symbols.

and the other the *prothesis,* the place where the Sacred Elements were reserved towards the end of the Liturgy.

The floor of the central nave and of the sanctuary, up as far as the altar, was covered with mosaic. The design was a simple geometrical one, but showed a cross at the entrance to the nave and another in front of the sanctuary. These latter may help in dating the building. By a decree of 427, the Christian Emperor, Theodosius II, banned the placing of crosses in church floors. If this decree was observed in churches of the Negev, then the East Church at Kurnub, with its crosses beneath, would be older than any other in the whole area. Later than the church, a small chapel and a baptistry were built close by. The font, unlike any other in the Negev churches, is sunk into the ground.

The other church at Kurnub, the Western, is a close reproduction of the Eastern one but in smaller dimensions: 30 meters long (including the atrium) by 17.5 wide. The salient feature of the building is the fact that most of its decoration has survived the centuries and we can see exactly what Byzantine Christians of the Negev could do with regard to artistry in columns, bases, door lintels, and other ornamented stonework. However, by far the most attractive element here is the wonderful mosaic which covers the floor of the central nave, right into the sanctuary, around the altar and up to the walls of the apse. In general, the design is geometrical, squares and circles; but these are decorated profusely with the figures of birds (including peacocks), baskets, and individual pieces of fruit (grapes, pomegranates, citrus and others which look like apples and figs). More interesting still are the five mosaic inscriptions of dedication in Greek which is still easily read, showing the name of Nilos twice: *Kyrie soson ton doulon sou Nilon ton philochriston ton ktisanta* ("Lord, save thy servant Nilos, the lover of Christ, who built this [place] and save, O Lord, this house, too"). The altar of the church was carefully removed, and only the marks of the base can be seen.

Other buildings in Kurnub, besides the churches, give evidence of the way of life of Christians there. Many doorposts and lintels, for example, show crosses and other symbols of the new faith. We are especially indebted for these findings to Dr. A. Negev who, on behalf of the Hebrew University, Jerusalem, and the Israel National Parks Authority, has brought this ancient city to light and interpreted much of its detail for us.

Graceful arch and lintel found near the Eastern Church, Kurnub.

JACOB'S WELL

IN THE LARGELY rainless lands of the Middle East, water is a constant preoccupation. This is brought home to us still by the fact that hundreds of place names there are simply those of springs, wells and oases. Thus, from Israel's Negev, west through Sinai, more than half the sites are called by something beginning with *Bir* (well) or *Ain* (spring). So it was in the early history of the Patriarchs, the first forebears of the Hebrew people. Their nomadic wanderings through Palestine were marked by sanctuaries, camps, and graves, but especially by places where they found water. Beersheba (Seven Wells, or Well of the Oath), where Abraham himself started an oasis, is the most famous (Genesis 21:22–34). Perhaps, the modern Israeli passion for tree-planting has its remote roots in him.

However, there was another well in central Palestine which, curiously enough, is not named in the Old Testament but is quite familiar from the New: Jacob's Well (Bir Ya'akov) in Samaria. Of old, the donor of such a well to a community was forever highly esteemed. In the Gospel story, the symbolic, but very real significance of Christ, the new Jacob, donor of water valid for eternal life, is brought out at length in the Fourth Gospel (John 4:1–42).

We are confident that we still know the exact site of this famous watering place. What St. John has to tell us fits in perfectly with the story of Jacob in the Old Testament. The Patriarch was returning from Mesopotamia to the traditional pasture-lands used by his people. He arrived "safe and sound at Sichem in the land of Canaan and camped in front of the town." Later, he established himself more permanently by purchasing a field, pitching his tents, and fashioning an altar to the divinity, adored as the God of Israel (Genesis 33:18–20). The spot was well known in tribal tradition, marked by a hoary terebinth tree where Jacob's grandfather, Abraham himself, had already built an altar (Genesis 12:6–7). In the background were the twin mountains of Ebal and Garizim, rising sheer from the surrounding plain, and later made famous by Joshua who dedicated here the Hebrew clans anew to the One God after their successful invasion of Canaan (Joshua 8:30–35). Jacob further earned the gratitude of both kinsfolk and strangers by digging a well and thereby ensuring a constant water supply for himself, his sons, and his flocks. The exact site of this well was the celebrated field later given by Jacob to his son Joseph, whose mummy was eventually brought back from Egypt to a final resting place here. There was a town close at hand, by name of Sichar.

The modern visitor will ask: where should we look for the town today? Why did Jacob dig a well when there were natural springs close by? Why did the Samaritan woman from the village come to draw water here? It is most likely that the town is to be identified with modern Askar, 65 kilometers north of Jerusalem, 150 meters east of modern Balata which contains the ruins of ancient Sichem. The well is shown about three hundred yards still further southeast. It is quite distinctive, being the only man-made one in the vicinity from which water has to be drawn by buckets. There is an important crossroads close by, and the visits of strangers like Jacob and other travellers watering their flocks at the town's water supply would not have been welcome. Hence, Jacob's thoughtful initiative in digging a new well would have been appreciated by visiting caravans and his name carried abroad gratefully through the land. In accord with the Gospel story, the townswoman would have sought water here because her menfolk were working in the fields nearby. It was near harvest time, and they were busy getting ready for the reaping (John 4:35).

The general background of the Gospel story remains the same and helps prove it genuine. With a gesture, the woman could point to the top of Mount Garizim quite close at hand, the peak where Samaritans worshipped, in place of Mount Zion (Jerusalem), from which they were excluded. The whole area was full of memories of the Patriarchs, and it was these traditions, mainly, which formed the basis of the Samaritan religion: "Our fathers worshipped on this mountain. . . ." (John 4:20).

In Christian tradition, the well and its surroundings were, of course, made famous by the meeting of Jesus and the woman. This was by far the most important Gospel event in Samaria, the foundation of the Christian community by Christ himself. One interested witness to it all was the apostle John, who subsequently not only wrote down the story but also came back as a Christian preacher to this same area, speaking in many villages of Samaria (Acts 8:25).

Another important writer who knew the place was St. Justin, who was born in Nablus, a few miles north of the well. He has left a note that Christians of Gentile origin in this area were more fervent and numerous than those whose background was Jewish or Samaritan. In the first half of the fourth century a bishop of Nablus, Germanus, took part in the Church Councils of 314 and 325. The presence of such a notable in the district implies a considerable number of Christians living near the shrine of Jacob's Well.

In 333, a French pilgrim from Bordeaux visited the place, and he was the first to make mention of a Christian sanctuary there. He tells us that it was the site of a sacred pool, and, from his use of this term elsewhere, it is clear that he means a baptistry. He makes no allusion to a church, so we can think of the well as having been left in its natural state. Moreover, we know from the story of ancient Nazareth that a baptistry could stand as a sacred monument in itself, without being attached to a regular church building. It would have been hard to find a better place for administering the first sacrament than the spot where Christ himself had spoken of divine gifts through the symbolism of well water.

In his guide to place names of the Holy Land, *Onomastikon,* Eusebius says that the famous well "is still pointed out." This means that there was a firm tradition at the spot, long before the liberation of Christians under Constantine (313). When St. Jerome came to translate the *Onomastikon* into Latin, he changed the above expression to "where a church is now built." This is the first mention of a formal church at Jacob's Well and, thanks to modern archaeology, we know something of its detail.

Built between 340 and 390, it was exactly cross-shaped, its architecture being influenced by the ancient baptistry which was most probably cruciform. There was a door at the end of each arm of the building and, in an open shallow crypt, was the main feature, Jacob's Well. Mosaic fragments of the north and west naves have come to light, as also trunks of ancient columns and parts of the walls. From these, scholars can calculate the size of this Byzantine building: about 30 meters over-all, with arms of about 9 meters each. Destroyed during Samaritan uprisings in 484 and 529, the church was restored by Emperor Justinian. At this time, the stone brink of the well was transferred to the basilica of Hagia Sophia in Constantinople, where it is still on view. The ancient church at Jacob's Well was destroyed about the tenth century A.D.

For the Crusaders, the well was a main point of interest, and they soon had a new and ample church built on the spot (1130). The largest of its three apses centered over the well itself, this being housed in a special chapel below floor level. Without the apses, the church measured 46 meters long, by 19 wide. It was known as "Saint Savior's," this title being derived from the confession of faith which climaxes the Gospel narrative: "This is indeed the Savior of the world" (John 4:42).

With the end of the Crusader kingdom, the church soon fell into ruin, much of its masonry being subsequently carried off and re-used by local people in their buildings. However, the solid stonework of the well in its crypt remained for centuries, though pilgrims often took home fragments as souvenirs. Others were accustomed to drink the well water, which was thought to have curative powers. Franciscan writers tell us that their confreres came once a year to the site to celebrate Mass, while the local farmers repaid the visit by selling grain from the surrounding fields to the religious in Jerusalem. By 1626, the Greek clergy were also visiting the ruins for liturgical ceremonies. In 1860, the Greek Orthodox Patriarch Cyril II bought the property, and soon excavations began to reveal the past history of the shrine. In 1966, the Franciscan archaeologist, Father Bellarmine Bagatti, published a report on all that has come to light so far, thanks to the courtesy of the present priest in charge, the Archimandrite Spiridion Scordillis.

To visit the shrine today, one must enter by a gate in the wall which surrounds the property. Inside, there is a lovely garden, well watered and always in flower. The main monument is the unfinished Greek church, with great fluted columns still waiting to be crowned by capitals and superstructure. This was begun in 1914, but work had to be stopped when funds from Russia ceased. It is hoped that the Orthodox Church of Greece will help to complete the building.

The apse of this new church stands over the crypt where the well itself is to be found. Lateral steps on each side go down to what is now a chapel, with the usual furnishings of an Eastern church, but without an iconostasis. Many votive lamps and other offerings hang from the ceiling. The well itself has a rose-stone and a square top, above which is the apparatus for drawing water in an aluminum bucket: a rope on a drum turned by a handle. The narrow opening of the mouth widens like a great bottle to the width of eight feet. The depth of the well has varied through the ages, mainly by reason of pilgrims throwing pebbles down to gage the water level and thereby sometimes blocking it completely. In 1955, it was cleared once again and found to go down 162 feet to the bottom. The water itself varies in depth, depending on the seasonal rains; it is not supplied by a real spring.

Sipping this water and re-reading the Gospel story, we are reminded of the deep symbolism of Christ's visit to this well and of his dialogue and discourse here. In the dry lands of the Middle East, it was natural that water should have been looked on as a sign of life, fertility and purification. Thus, at the beginning of the Bible, Eden is pictured as an oasis with abundant streams and luxurious vegetation. It became a pattern, often used in the Scriptures, to describe God's eventual salvation of the Jewish people and of all men. The Lord himself was known as a living spring, as the good shepherd who provides water for his flock. In the great climax of redemption, water was to flow from the Temple of Jerusalem and to accompany a new outpouring of God's spirit in the world.

About the time of Christ's appearance, especially, the well or spring was given a high symbolic sense. It was hoped that the three wells or springs known to the Hebrews in their wandering through the desert—Miriam's, Moses', and that of the Princes—would provide wonderful water once more, namely in the time of the Messiah's coming, and through the intercession of Elijah. The recluses of Qumran spoke of the mouth of the Master of Justice as a well of informed teaching, stimulating many arid minds. They also knew the symbolism of the "well of the Princes" and the hopes associated with it. St. Paul has a clear allusion to the well or spring of Moses (1 Corinthians 10:4). One Jewish commentary on its symbolism was that Moses struck the rock twice, the first time producing blood, the second time, water. This tradition is referred to by St. John when he describes blood and water gushing from the side of Christ just after he "gave up the spirit" (John 19:34f.).

It is St. John, too, who describes Christ, in the very precincts of the Temple, promising to give new water to the world, namely, by providing a fresh outpouring of God's Spirit (John 7:37–39). At the end of the New Testament, John neatly completes the Bible with a description of Paradise restored, using once more the symbolism of the oasis that is found at the beginning of Genesis: "Then he showed me the river of the water of life, bright as crystal, flowing from the throne of God and of the Lamb . . . " (Revelation 22:1–2). St. John's deep interest in Samaria and his understanding of water symbolism in the Scriptures gives fuller meaning to his account of Christ promising the waters of eternal life at a well in central Israel. It is useful to ponder his message once more, standing by the brink of Jacob's Well.

Belfry of the unfinished church, Jacob's Well.

JERUSALEM

The Basilica of the Holy Sepulcher

IN ALL THE Holy Land, the most hallowed church is that of the Holy Sepulcher, Jerusalem, the scene of Christ's glorification in his passion, death and resurrection. It should be the most marvelous Christian building on earth as it had, indeed, been in the distant past. Instead, it is, comparatively speaking, the shabbiest. I have officially received many visitors here and guided them to the focal sanctuary. The look of dismay and disappointment on many faces, when told that this is the climax of their long pilgrimage, is often quite pathetic. However, there is no point dwelling on the very plain and presently unchangeable facts. In visiting or studying the basilica, as it is now, two things are called for, and the first is faith.

Like the Eucharist, the most solemn Christian act proclaiming Christ's glorification, the basilica is in itself a "mystery of faith." As we shall see, history and archaeology confirm that faith, but the monuments themselves remain merely material structures unless they take on a sacramental value for us—unless they effectively put us in touch with God and his grace. In other words, we must penetrate the inner meaning of the stone, marble and mosaic that we see here. The very fact the building has to be propped up by unsightly steel and wooden struts forces us to do just that. More than anywhere else in the world are we starkly reminded of the very purpose of a church: a place for prayer, a place for instruction. The description we offer in these pages is designed to guide this approach, to stimulate faith, and, perhaps, to elicit prayer here on the site of *the* great Christian mystery.

A second requirement in studying the basilica of the Holy Sepulcher as it stands is that of sympathy. Here one is in contact with remains of the past which have often been repaired, but rarely transformed. The obvious reason for this is that people here resist change. This is the more so because change in the past has nearly always been for the worse. Christian communities have been deprived of their historic rights, and some of them have even disappeared. The monument itself has been pillaged, burnt, and leveled to the ground. It is no wonder that a deep yearning for some kind of stability has gradually developed, and that the principle of the *Status Quo* has come to govern the order of worship. A survey of the story of the basilica brings out the reason for these facts. It also helps us to

Façade of the Basilica of the Holy Sepulcher, Jerusalem.   93

take a charitable view of the widely differing practices we witness. Above all, it brings us to sympathize with the human personalities who here still proclaim the religious mystery of Christ's death and of his empty grave.

There is no doubt that we know the actual site where Christ died and was entombed. The interest of the first Christians in these events and in the places where they occurred is best illustrated by our founding documents themselves, the Gospels, where the four writers come together in presenting carefully and in great detail the narrative of the passion, death and resurrection. This same memory was very much alive in 135 A.D. as is emphasized by the fact that, after crushing the last Jewish rebellion against the Romans in Palestine, Emperor Hadrian set about demolishing the main centers of upheaval by turning them into a Roman city strewn with pagan temples. Thus, not only did the purely Jewish area of the Temple disappear, but also the places held sacred by Judaeo-Christians. Actually, it was the whole area around Calvary that was transformed into the Capitol of Roman Jerusalem, which the Romans re-named Aelia Capitolina, the Christian shrines being literally buried beneath it. Hadrian's scheme proved unsuccessful. Instead of blotting out the memory of where Christ had died, he actually succeeded in perpetuating it. In a city which in time became largely pagan, it was "Hebrews"—that is, Judaeo-Christians—who preserved the traditions associated with Calvary and the tomb.

During the Council of Nicaea (325), the Bishop of Jerusalem, Macarius, approached the Emperor Constantine and persuaded him that the most sacred Christian places should be sought out once more. A kind of archaeological expedition ensued, the site immediately chosen for examination being the one known by tradition. The results have been described with almost delirious enthusiasm by Eusebius, Bishop of Caesarea. Digging deep down into the virgin soil, the excavators soon came across the Christian shrines and, "beyond all hope," found them almost intact: "the most holy cave . . . the venerable and most hallowed witness to the resurrection of the Savior." Modern archaeology confirms all this, and, despite some obscurity which still persists regarding the direction of the ancient city walls, we can be confident that we know the place of Christ's death and burial as described in the Gospels. "I am more sure of the tomb of Jesus being here than I am of the tomb of Napoleon in the Invalides," said an eminent French archaeologist, Père Vincent, a Dominican.

Emperor Constantine was not content only with investigating the past. He decreed also that a fitting memorial to the great mysteries be built by free Christians

94

Via Dolorosa, Jerusalem. Ecce Homo arch in rear.

over the traditional places. Modern architects sometimes try to fit a new building into the surrounding site. Constantine ruthlessly adopted the opposite course: clear the site to ennoble the new structure. He had this done twice, once on the Vatican hill in Rome where it took seven years to prepare the ground for the first basilica of St. Peter, and, again, in Jerusalem around the Holy Sepulcher and Calvary.

The tomb in which Christ's body was laid was a fairly elaborate one, as befitted the aristocratic station of Joseph of Arimathea. There was, first, a fairly spacious anteroom cut from the rock, where relatives could gather on anniversaries. The burial chamber proper was farther in, and it was entered through a low door. The entrance to the inner room was sealed by a great stone which could be wheeled across the opening. Constantine's engineers took the entrance to the inner chamber as their level and freed the whole tomb from the surrounding rock, demolishing even the antechamber, much to the regret of modern scholars.

Then they turned to Calvary. This is nowhere called a "mount" in the Gospels, but simply a "place," a prominent place such as is still named in the Semitic languages *ras* ("head" or "prominence"). The particular turn of phrase used in this instance was *Golgotha* ("skull"), in Latin, *Calvaria* ("bald head"). Only after Constantine's men had cut free the mound from the surrounding rock did it get the designation "mount."

The full design of Constantine's basilica provided a gradual, majestic introduction by architecture to the central mysteries of Christianity. The entrance was from the great main thoroughfare, the "Broadway" which Hadrian had imperiously cut straight through the old city of Jerusalem. Turning westward from this (all of Constantine's basilicas faced east), one entered the first atrium by one of three doors, the remains of which are still to be seen. This area was surrounded by columns, with a fountain for ritual purposes in the middle. Then one entered the basilica proper, the *Martyrium* of Christ, 45 meters long by 26 wide, with five naves, an apse and an altar at the end. Beneath this building was a crypt which later in history became associated with St. Helena and the finding of the true cross. Side galleries connected the *Martyrium* with another cloister which had as its main feature the "mount" of Calvary to the left (south). Finally, one came to the most hallowed place of all, the *Anastasis,* or site of Christ's resurrection.

The style adopted was that of the classical Roman mausoleum: a circle of columns supporting a dome over the tomb. However, as recent excavations (1961–62) show, Constantine's architect did not follow through the full detail by placing another circle of columns around the first eighteen. Instead, he only half completed this outer row, thus creating a great half-dome or arching shell. Even the regular lines of this were diversified by polygonal sides and especially by three apses, one at each front end and another in the back center. The area

Stone of the Anointing, Holy Sepulcher Basilica.

left free by the incomplete outer circle was used for assembly purposes, and thence visitors could walk around the ambulatory surrounding the tomb in the mausoleum proper.

The whole was enclosed on the east by a façade which was entered from the Calvary foyer, as already mentioned. Twenty great windows let in a flood of light, reflected on the marble walls and lamps of gold and silver, and this in itself was a symbol of the resurrection, the victory of light over darkness. Unfortunately, this feature is no longer in existence. The tomb itself was in the shape of a cone or pyramid, such as is still seen in funerary monuments in the Kidron valley. In time, it was so heavily covered with ornaments and votive offerings that the color of its limestone rock could no longer be discerned.

To the north, west and south of the Rotunda, Constantine's engineers cut further into the surrounding hill and there constructed dwellings and utility buildings for the Patriarch and clergy serving the basilica. The most recent excavations on this site (1961–62) have brought to light much of the detail here, including wine and oil presses and storage rooms for jars.

Three centuries of Byzantine peace in Palestine came to an end with the Persian invasions of 614. The rampaging troops of Chosroes concentrated their fury on the basilica of the Holy Sepulcher and soon it was a smoking heap of ashes, its stout walls alone resisting total destruction. The Patriarch and the notables of the city were made captive, and all the ornaments of the churches were carried off as booty. However, in 629, with the victory of Heraclius, Christians returned to Jerusalem and the work of reconstruction began. Modestus, the Superior of a desert monastery, had become Patriarch of Jerusalem, and to him we owe the first restoration of the basilica. Constantine's design was followed faithfully so that, in general, the plan of the church remained the same. Modestus' main work consisted in restoring roofs and refurbishing decorations.

The comparatively peaceful period of the Moslem occupation (beginning in 638) allowed Christians to worship publicly in the basilica and other churches. There were even periods of prosperity when Western pilgrims visited in large numbers. In Charlemagne's time, a group of one hundred and fifty persons served the shrine. On the other hand, there were occasional difficulties, and eventually these culminated in the infamous order of Caliph Hakim of Cairo: "destroy without trace the church of the *Qiame* [Resurrection] and root up its very foundations." The work of demolition began on October 18, 1009, but the walls again proved too strong. Nevertheless, the building was totally pillaged and the rock above the tomb of Christ disappeared. More serious was the damage to the *Martyrium* or basilica proper. This was so great that the edifice was never rebuilt. As a result, only the abbreviated, west end of the original church has come down to our own time.

The ledge where Jesus was laid to rest.

The second reconstruction was undertaken by another Constantine, Monomachus. His architects concentrated on the Rotunda, reinforcing the columns still standing and building a new dome of stone. To support this great weight, they were forced to block up windows in the upper galleries, and the building began to lose some of its charm. They repaired the façade and floor, refurbishing the walls with marble. The most notable additions were four side chapels around the Rotunda, to compensate for the loss of the *Martyrium*, which was never replaced. These oratories are still in use today. The work of repair undertaken by Monomachus took six years to complete (1042–1048).

Some fifty years later, Godfrey de Bouillon led the triumphant Crusader armies into Jerusalem (July 15, 1099), and a new era in the story of the basilica opened. The Crusader passion for architecture and building, which mounted almost to a fever in Palestine, focused above all on the site of the Holy Sepulcher. The architects took over the existing plan of Monomachus, but embellished it greatly. The main work was that of organization and unification. Thus, all the former shrines were brought under one roof. The ancient, second foyer (by now referred to as "the garden") was turned into a regular choir, with a central and two side naves. Corresponding to these, three great doors were opened in the façade of the Rotunda, and thus one unified church in the Roman cathedral style was created. For the first time, too, Calvary was included in the one building, thus reducing the site of the passion and resurrection to a very modest scale in the eyes of the modern visitor. The tomb itself was housed in an artistic little temple, while the walls of the three distinctive shrines—the Rotunda, Calvary, and the Crypt of St. Helena's—were highly decorated with marble, inscriptions and paintings commemorating the central mysteries. For the first time, a bell tower was added, a three-storied structure crowned with a small eight-sided dome, which was the work of a Spaniard, Jordano, and which is reminiscent of such towers still to be seen in Catalonia, Spain. The solemn consecration of the whole basilica took place on July 15, 1149, the fiftieth anniversary of the Crusader occupation of Jerusalem.

To a contemporary Moslem writer, Idrisi, who saw the church in 1154, the Crusader basilica was "one of the marvels of the world." More remarkable, perhaps, than the material monument was the generous way in which the Crusaders proved themselves ecumenical, faithful to universal Christian tradition. So far as was possible, they kept all the main features of the former (Eastern) construction, took over customs in use at the time, wrote their inscriptions in both Greek and Latin, and left the rites of the Orientals intact so that the latter were free to worship at their own altars in peace. Unfortunately, the subsequent story of the basilica, up till quite recent days, is one of deterioration in almost every respect.

In 1808, a disastrous fire destroyed the central nave of the Crusader church

100

and the Rotunda, bringing down in ruins the large dome. In the task of rebuilding, which began in 1810, the Western Church had no part, all Europe being more concerned with the Napoleonic Wars. The Greek architect, Comninos of Mitylene, has been harshly judged by posterity for his work in obscuring the former clear lines of the building by introducing heavy, dull pilasters, erecting many dividing walls, and blocking up most windows. The lack of taste in this whole reconstruction is unfortunately still displayed in the *edicule,* or little chapel, over the tomb, the central but most miserable feature of the modern basilica.

In 1927, another disaster struck the church, this time in the form of an earthquake which nearly brought down the whole structure. The Mandatory Power of the time (Great Britain) tried to organize a massive reconstruction effort on the part of the various Christian communities concerned with the preservation of the priceless monument, but in vain. Finally, despairing of any kind of cooperation, the authorities in 1935 bound together the remains with steel and wooden scaffolding. While annually torturing the structure in the changes of Jerusalem's temperatures, the remedy was ultimately successful in the sense that the building still stands. At last, on May 27, 1959, there came a great day when the interested communities, Greeks, Latins and Armenians, committed themselves to a partial restoration of the existing basilica. This work continues, limited to the areas held in particular by the various religious bodies, leaving the reconstruction of the central shrine of the Rotunda still problematical. In 1949, plans for a great basilica on this site had been drawn up and modeled in miniature by the Latins, but the plans remain a dream to be realized in the distant future.

PERSONNEL

On entering the basilica, the visitor is soon struck by the different dress of the priests and religious to be seen on all sides. However, this is nothing compared to his surprise when he assists at a sacred service and is often distracted by the liturgical celebrations going on simultaneously at another altar, sometimes in chant which just does not harmonize. This is normal in Jerusalem, where clergy of different rites live together; but it is most striking in the Basilica of the Holy Sepulcher where occasionally personnel of five different rites worship at the same time. Nineteen chapels are in their charge, while around the Rotunda and in the nearby buildings they have their own permanent lodgings.

Three major communities hold the basilica in common ownership: the Latins (represented by the Franciscans), the Greek Orthodox, and the Armenian Orthodox. There are two other rites that are permitted to celebrate on certain days within the church: the Coptic Orthodox, and the Syrian Orthodox. Monks of the Abys-

sinian (Ethiopian) rite actually live on the roof of the crypt, but they do not enter for religious ceremonies. The Anglicans occasionally worship in the adjoining Greek Orthodox chapel close to the basilica proper.

The Greek Orthodox are members of the Confraternity of the Holy Sepulcher, an ancient brotherhood organized towards the end of the sixteenth century and concerned with guarding the sanctuaries held by their Church, training members of the higher clergy, caring for parishes, deciding legal cases, and administering the property of their Patriarchate. Their dress is a long, black soutane with ample sleeves. Their hair is worn long, in a bun at the back of the neck, and their distinctive headgear is a cylindrical, brimless, black hat. Of the ten religious attached to the Holy Sepulcher, the Superior lives in the chapel of St. Abraham to the right of the church square; the others live on the ground floor behind the church. The main church within the basilica, called the *Katholikon,* is the Greek Orthodox cathedral of Jerusalem. The religious also administer half the area on Calvary and the Chapel of Adam beneath, and also chapels commemorating stages in the Passion of Christ—those of The Prison, St. Longinus, The Mocking, and The Crowning with Thorns. The form of worship consists of morning and afternoon prayer, but most of the services are held at night, especially now with the work of reconstruction going on all day. At 11:30 p.m., there is a long recitation of psalms, followed by Liturgy about 1:00 a.m. in the *Katholikon.* The altar, however, is placed in the vestibule of the Holy Sepulcher (Chapel of the Angel), atop a small marble column there. At other times, the Liturgy is performed on Calvary, above the spot where Christ's cross was fixed.

The Liturgy is taken from one of three ritual forms, that of St. Basil, of St. John Chrysostom, or of St. Gregory. The chant is distinctive, and the faithful follow with fervor, signing themselves frequently with a triple sign of the Cross. This is made with the first three fingers of the hand, in honor of the Trinity, and the right shoulder is touched first, before the left. Numerous incensations and an abundance of decoration—lamps, candles, icons and other sacred objects—make for a service which is quite rich by Western standards. However, assisting intelligently at such services, one feels oneself in contact with a great depth of Christianity, especially with the mentality of the early Church Fathers and Councils, not always the case in the practical and often hurried liturgy of the West.

The Armenian Orthodox religious form a community of three or four, living above the main door of the basilica. Their dress is quite distinctive, consisting of a black soutane and, over this, a black hood and long scapular, the head being always covered in public with the cowl. They are under the direction of the Patriarch, who lives at the Church of St. James on Mount Zion, near the Jaffa Gate. Like the Greeks, they begin their services about 11:30 at night but have to wait for the former to finish before beginning their own Mass about 2:30 or 3:00 a.m. Their altar is the marble slab over the tomb of Christ. The Liturgy is a fusion of the rites of St. James and of St. John Chrysostom, simpler than the Greek and closer in many ways to the Latin. Their chant is continuous, melodic and haunting, embellished by the use of bells, cymbals and gongs. The liturgical dress of all the ministers is ample and colorful (always spotlessly clean, too). Three times weekly, they begin a procession around the main shrines of the basilica just as the Latins have nearly finished theirs. They have a chapel in their residence above the arches of the Rotunda, and also administer the Chapel of the Division of the Raiment (Christ's garments). However, their main center is the historic crypt below the whole basilica, known as the Chapel of St. Helena or the Church of the Holy Cross. Here, from the fourth to the seventh centuries, the famous relic of the Cross was worshipped, and the antiquity of the building enhances its charm.

The Latin rite is represented by the Franciscans. They are paid a continuous compliment by the other communities in that the Orthodox would not tolerate their being changed for any other Roman Catholic body whatsoever. Their dress is familiar to most Western Christians: brown tunic and cowl, white cord, open sandals. Their presence in the Holy Land goes back to the time of their founder, St. Francis, who personally visited Palestine in 1219 and, from Acre, supervised the setting up of the first "overseas Province" of his followers. Despite the final defeat of the Crusaders, the Franciscans never disbanded this Province but stayed on as the official guardians of most of the shrines still held here by the Latin Church.

In joining the Holy Sepulcher community, a Franciscan takes on the most difficult charge in the Holy Land. The program of dinner at 10:00 a.m. and supper at 5:00 p.m. is geared to the fact that the Office of Matins is said—or sometimes sung—at midnight. Private Masses begin at 4:00 a.m., and the whole community sings the public Mass at the Holy Sepulcher at 7:00 a.m. With the work of reconstruction going on, the day is filled with the sound of chisel on stone, with fine dust penetrating everywhere. Nevertheless, religious ceremonies are carried out, notably the procession to the various chapels of the basilica at 4:00 p.m., the order of this being at least five hundred years old.

The ceremonies of Holy Week are performed with great solemnity. One peculiarity, however, is that the "new" Latin ritual and horarium of 1954 cannot be followed because of conflict with the basilica's constitution, the *Status Quo,* the main tenor of which is, simply, "no change." The para-liturgical rite of the "Funeral of Christ" on Good Friday has long attracted the devotion of Catholics, ending as it does with the placing of the statue of the dead Christ within the tomb itself. The Franciscans have their own little church where the Blessed Sacrament is reserved, a part of Calvary area, the pillar marking the appearance of Christ to St. Mary Magdalene, and the grotto of the Finding of the Cross beneath the Armenian church.

The Coptic Orthodox are Christians who originated in Egypt (their name coming from the Greek *Guptos*, "Egyptian"), and separated from Rome in 451 over a theological difference concerning the nature of Christ. In Jerusalem, they are under the direction of a bishop whose residence is close outside the apse of the basilica. About fifteen in number, the Coptic clergy are normally dependent ultimately on their Patriarch in Cairo. They wear a black soutane covered with a mantle with wide sleeves. A black leather girdle and a flat, black cap, something like a very formal beret, make them distinctive. Since 1573, they have functioned in the basilica in a small chapel at the rear (west) end of the edicule over the tomb. For religious on duty, there are two rooms within the precincts of the church. Three times a week they hold services. Their Sunday morning Office is very long, beginning at 4:30 and, unfortunately, overlapping the Latin Mass sung at 7:00. The Liturgy follows either the ancient rite of St. Cyril of Alexandria, or the formulae of the Greeks, St. Gregory and St. Basil.

The fifth community, the Syrian Orthodox, are under the direction of the Patriarch of Antioch. They have a bishop in Jerusalem, in the Residence of St. Mark which is believed to be the house of Mary, Mark's mother, where St. Peter took refuge after his deliverance from prison (Acts 12:12). During ceremonies, the Syrians are easily recognized by the black kerchief with colored crosses drawn tightly over the head. Their chapel is a hidden, lowly place in the central apse of the original Constantine basilica, just across from the Coptic chapel adjoining the edicule. With some variations, they follow the rite of the Church of Antioch, dating back to the fourth century.

Being human and widely separated by background, language and custom, these various Christian communities have had their differences from time to time. However, it is petty to dwell on such things when the very presence of these same people, often literally locked up together in the one building, represents a faith and steadfastness which is little short of heroic. The very doors of the basilica are still under the control of two Moslem janitors, but the interior, with all the splendor of various liturgies, is quite Christian indeed. It is the resident communities who continue to bring life, meaning, and grace to the great monument. Without them, it would long since have stood simply as a silent museum.

THE SHRINES

Visiting the Church of the Holy Sepulcher for the first time, one is struck by the smallness of it all. It is important to remember its long history and to realize that now we actually have to pass through a side door into what remains of the biggest building ever constructed in Christian Jerusalem. If one is sufficiently energetic,

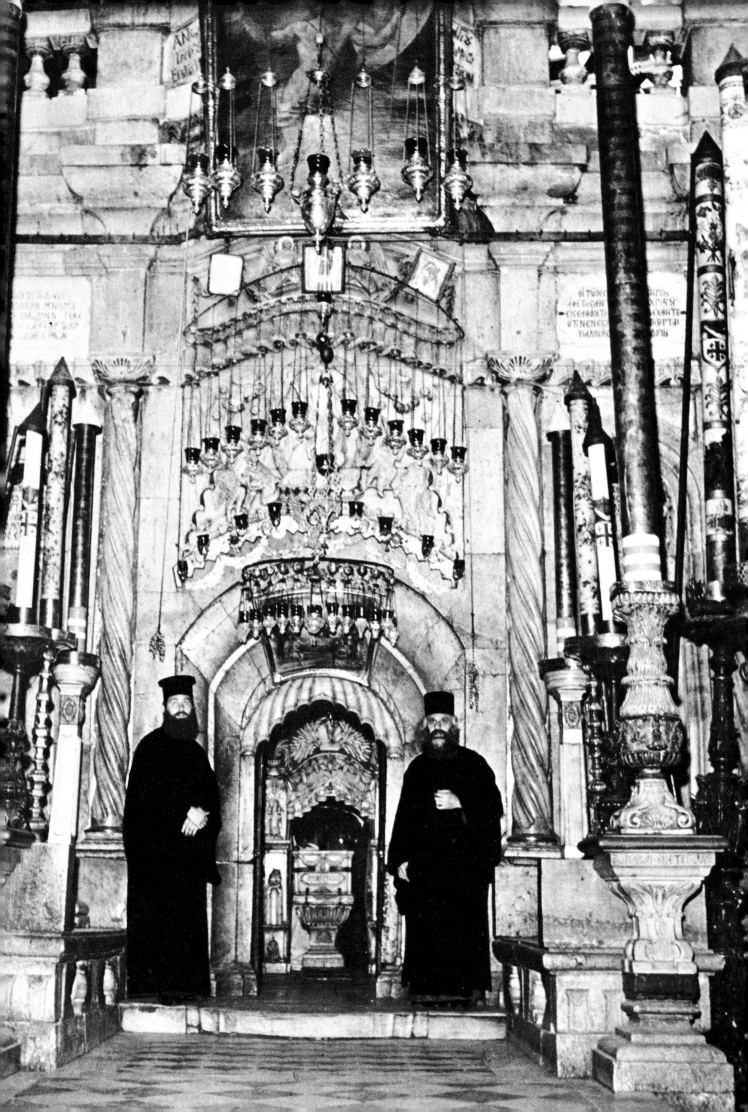

one can climb to the top of the Lutheran church-tower nearby and get a good idea of the former dimensions. Looking from left to right (west to east), the two larger domes are followed by a small one, above the subterranean Chapel of St. Helena, while a fourth little cupola leads the eye on farther to a church with nine windows. This latter marks the original entrance to the ancient Constantine basilica, its over-all length having been one hundred and fifteen meters.

The modern entrance is fronted by a little square where religious buildings huddle close to the church itself. In the twelfth century, the courtyard was covered over, and the butts of the columns of this portico can still be seen. On the left are the apses of three Greek Orthodox chapels, those of St. James, St. John, and the Forty Martyrs. On the right of the square is the Orthodox chapel of St. Abraham, the Armenian chapel of St. John, and the Coptic chapel of St. Michael. The façade of the basilica has kept its Crusader character. There are two doors with corresponding windows above, ornamented by small columns with capitals of acanthus leaves. The door to the right is sealed. The official opening of the other is a ceremonial in itself, a ladder being used to reach the actual lock. The belfry to the left of the entrance is the truncated tower built by Jordano, from which the topmost story disappeared in 1549. On the right of the entrance is a flight of twelve steps leading up to a stately Crusader door which is still richly adorned with capitals and carvings of vine leaves and grapes. It formerly opened into the sacred shrine of Calvary and, from the height of the stairway, we already get some idea of why the term "mount" Calvary came into use. Today, the door is permanently closed and the area immediately behind has been transformed into the Latin Chapel of our Lady of Sorrows (or Chapel of the Franks).

Passing through the door of the basilica, one sees first the Stone of the Anointing, a slab of red marble, almost at ground level and inscribed with Greek lettering commemorating the hasty embalming of Christ's body after it had been brought down from Calvary (John 19:40). In Byzantine times, there was a small chapel here, the oratory of St. Mary, but it was demolished during the Crusader reconstructions.

A little further on to the left is another memorial which the casual visitor may miss. It is in the form of a round stone surrounded by an iron framework, and it probably represents some ancient feature connected with the chapel of St. Mary. Today, it is associated with the faithful womenfolk who stood at a distance from Calvary watching Christ being done to death (Matthew 27:55–56). It is the property of the Armenian Orthodox, whose sacristy is just to the left, while the stairs nearby lead up to their residence and chapel.

Suddenly, we enter the area of the Rotunda, once so marvelous, the climax of a much more gradual approach in the full plan of the basilica. The unfortunate features of the reconstruction of 1810 are only too evident, a circumstance ag-

Façade of the edicule housing the Tomb.

gravated by the unsightly wooden scaffolding in place since 1935. This is the time to recall the former delicate shape of the mausoleum and the richness of its lavish decoration. In the center is the most sacred feature of the whole basilica, the edicule, or small chapel, housing the tomb of Christ. In length, it measures 8.30 meters, in width and height, 5.90. Around its sides, sixteen pillars frame arched panels and support a balustrade of small columns above. A miniscule dome in the onion-shaped, Moscovite style crowns all. The front is flanked by rows of large candlesticks, the property of the major communities worshipping here. The façade of the edicule is over-decorated with lamps and pictures, while the inscriptions in Greek are prayers to the Risen Christ, as light triumphant over darkness.

Inside, we find an anteroom, corresponding to the more elaborate form of Jewish burial places. As already remarked, the original chamber was removed by Constantine's builders. This compartment is now called the Chapel of the Angel, and the decorations remind us of the story of the appearance of the angel to the women on the first Easter morning. The abbreviated names of Mary (mother of James), Salome, Mary Magdalene, and the archangel Gabriel are inscribed. The Greek text flowing over the doorway is a reference to Luke 24:5: "Why do you seek the living among the dead?"

In the middle of the chapel, a small pedestal is fixed, and on top of this is a piece of masonry traditionally held to be a fragment of the circular stone which was used to close the entrance to the tomb proper. On this the angel was seated when the women appeared. The column is still used as the base of the Greek Orthodox altar when that liturgy is celebrated here.

A small doorway, only 1.33 meters high, leads into the burial chamber, the Holy Sepulcher proper. On the right is a marble slab, much smaller than we might expect, 2.07 meters long, 1.93 wide, and raised 66 cm. from the floor. It marks the ledge where the body of Christ was laid. The marble covering has been in place since 1555, when the Franciscan Superior, Boniface of Ragusa, replaced the Crusader chapel with another. Pictures, lamps, candlesticks and inscriptions feature aspects of the Resurrection mystery. Amongst the engravings is the name of the Greek architect, Comninos of Mitylene, who is responsible for the present small temple.

Coming out of the edicule, one may walk straight ahead to visit the main church of the basilica, the Greek Orthodox cathedral called the Katholikon. The congregation stands here when the Liturgy is sung at the altar within the Chapel of the Angel. The Katholikon is lavishly decorated in the Eastern style, and its appearance has been greatly enhanced by the renovation of the four great columns and the arches supporting the dome. A special item of interest is the little white marble hemisphere beneath the cupola, showing Jerusalem as the hub of the world, with Europe, Asia and Africa as its radii. It recalls the belief, stated frequently in the Psalms, that God has made Jerusalem the center of all his work on earth. In Psalm 48:2, Jerusalem is "the joy of all the earth, Mount Zion, in the far north, the city of the great King." Christians transferred many details of this tradition to the site of the Resurrection.

Walking back to the edicule, one may pass right around it and find at the back a small, dark chapel attached to the west end, that of the Coptic Orthodox who worship here three times a week. A religious will light a candle and show, beneath the altar, the actual stone of Christ's tomb, bare of marble. In 1048, the Emperor Constantine Monomachus built the altar for the parish of Jerusalem, and it was kept by the Crusaders, who gave it the name *Cavet,* "head," for it seemed to form the head of the whole monument of the edicule. Removed but later restored again, it was handed over to the Copts at the request of Mehemet Ali, their protector in Egypt.

Leaving this chapel, one goes straight forward between two of the great columns of the Rotunda into a very obscure room which, though it is called the Chapel of the Syrians, is actually the property of the Armenians. Here another ancient Liturgy is occasionally celebrated. On the left of this chapel there is a narrow door leading into a still darker chamber which has been given the name of Tomb of Joseph of Arimathea. There is clear evidence that this was a Jewish burial ground and this, in its own way, confirms the fact that we do still know the site of Christ's tomb. There is question of a cemetery area outside Jerusalem proper, for Jews never buried their dead within the city walls. It was part of the general locality where Joseph of Arimathea owned property, a kind of garden area which was never built up—possibly because the top-soil was too deep since it was actually the filling of an ancient quarry. This is the reason for the closeness of the next shrine in the basilica, to the northeast and outside the row of columns of the Rotunda: the Latin Chapel of the Appearance to St. Mary Magdalene. It commemorates the story of Mary's meeting with the "Gardener" (John 20:15), and the hymn sung here during the daily procession to the shrines is appropriate and charming.

Slightly to the north and further along, the little church of the Latins is in view. It is a memorial to a tradition nowhere mentioned in the Scriptures, but of long standing, that Jesus appeared to his mother soon after the Resurrection. The Chapel of Mary in this locality is ancient, having been added by Constantine Monomachus in the eleventh century. The present building has been tastefully refurbished, and re-opened for worship in 1965. Westerners will like its comparative austerity and feel at home before the simple altar and its modest tabernacle. On the side altar to the right is shown a porphyry column, three quarters of a meter high, which is venerated as the Column of the Flagellation, the pillar to which Christ was tied during his scourging.

Leaving this chapel one sees, next, on the left, the door to the Latin sacristy. The main item of interest in that room is the glass case on the wall containing a sword and a pair of spurs, said to have belonged to the Crusader leader, Godfrey of Bouillon. These are still used as symbolic insignia when Knights of the Holy Sepulcher are created. Behind the sacristy and chapel is the residence of the Franciscans with apartments on various levels but having as its most pleasant feature a little terrace on the roof where, in this closely built-up quarter, the religious can relax in peace in God's fresh air.

Leaving the Latin sacristy, one turns to the left to visit the several chapels around the Katholikon, all of which commemorate some aspect of Christ's passion. As already noted, these were added to the basilica to compensate for the loss of the *Martyrium,* destroyed by Caliph Hakim. In succession, one sees the Prison of Christ, the Chapel of St. Longinus, the Chapel of the Division of the Raiment, and the Chapel of the Mocking. Disregarding, for the moment, the great stairway downward, one comes across a flight of eighteen very narrow steps which lead up to Calvary. The main stairway is further on after a turn to the left, back near the main door of the basilica. It is more convenient to ascend by this.

Five meters above the floor of the basilica, the area of Calvary is 11.45 meters long by 9.25 wide. It is divided into two naves by two great pillars. The chapel on the right (south) is tended by the Franciscans, the other by the Greek-Orthodox. The Latin chapel stands in what was once the foyer of Crusader Calvary, where the ceiling and walls were decorated with gleaming gold mosaics. In 1937, the present chapel was entirely renovated and something of the former glory of the mosaics has been restored. The main picture above the altar shows Christ being nailed to the cross in sight of his mother. The expression of intolerable grief, yet of majestic self-control, is quite wonderfully brought out in Mary's face. Other representations are those of the faithful women watching the crucifixion and of the offering of Isaac in sacrifice by his father, Abraham. Panels in the altar itself also show scenes from Christ's passion. This altar, made in Italy in 1588, was originally intended to stand by the Stone of the Anointing when the latter was held by the Franciscans alone.

Between the altar and the Greek area is a small bust of Our Lady of Sorrows, belonging to the Latins; it was brought from Lisbon in 1778 and represents the prophetic words of Simeon to Mary, "and a sword shall pierce through your own soul also" (Luke 2:35). The image is covered with various kinds of ornaments and votive offerings. (In 1967, particular attention was drawn to this sculpture when, on August 2, a tiara of precious stones was stolen from the head. The greater part of the jewelry was recovered and solemnly restored by the Israeli police on September 26.) The little altar was renovated in 1937, and a part of the original rock of Calvary was exposed under glass.

The main part of Calvary is crowned by the third altar to the left (north), tended by the Greeks and richly decorated with lamps, candlesticks and votive gifts. The central feature is found beneath the columns supporting the altar: a silver disc around an opening which commemorates the place where the shaft of Christ's cross was fixed. On each side, circles of black marble mark the site where the two thieves were executed at the same time (Mark 15:27). On the right-hand side of the altar is a fissure in the rock which runs through and can be seen also from the chapel beneath. It is associated with the report that, as Christ died, "the earth shook and the rocks were split" (Matthew 27:51).

Coming down from Calvary, you may visit this chapel underneath called the Chapel of Adam, which is especially rich in Christian symbolism. Catholics as well as Greeks are familiar with crucifixes bearing a skull or crossbar beneath the figure of the dead Christ. This custom originated with the Judaeo-Christians' habit of transferring many of the ancient traditions identifying Jerusalem as the hub of the world to the Calvary area. One such tradition was that Adam, the biblical father of the human race, was buried beneath the rock of Calvary and that, on the day of redemption, the blood of Christ first fell on him. Here also there were memories of the sacrifice of Melchizedek (Genesis 14:18) as well as of Abraham's offering of Isaac (Genesis 22). The present altar is actually dedicated to Melchizedek. To the left of this chapel—which once belonged to the now extinct Christians of Nubia—is the sacristy of the Greeks, where, with the permission of the Superior, one may see the age-old liturgical treasury, with its beautifully designed vestments, miters and reliquaries, and the sword of Peter the Great of Russia.

One final and important section of the basilica is to be noted: the crypt, which is associated, by long-standing pious tradition and devotion in Christian life, with the finding of the true cross of Christ. To reach it, one must return to the back of the Katholikon and go down a broad flight of twenty-nine steps. Here is a regular church with three naves, divided by pillars which are obviously ancient. Carpets, tapestries, and paintings depicting scenes from Armenian church history, remind us that this is the center of worship of the Armenian Orthodox. One particular feature is the great number of small, regular crosses cut in the walls by generations of pilgrims testifying to the fact that they had completed their long journey and symbolic of their special worship in this place. The church is called officially the Church of the Holy Cross, but more commonly it is known as the Church of St. Helena. The chief altar is dedicated to her. The other, to the left, is sacred to St. Dismas, who died on a cross at Christ's side and who received from him the gracious assurance, "Truly, I say to you, today you will be with me in Paradise" (Luke 23:43). The third nave leads, not to another apse and altar, but to a further flight of thirteen steps, down into the lowest chamber of the basilica,

An Eastern rite priest celebrating the Liturgy.

the Latin Chapel of the Finding of the Cross. Here, according to a tradition which goes back to the fourth century, the instruments of torture and the crosses used in the death of Christ and his companions were hastily thrown just before the Sabbath began. St. Ambrose (395) is the first to mention the tradition that it was St. Helena, mother of Constantine the Great, who found the true cross of Christ. Rufinus (420) tells the story of the cure of a dying man when touched with it. From the mid-fourth century onward, the veneration of the True Cross became a feature of Christian worship at the basilica and, throughout the Christian world, fragments were taken far and wide and treasured as sacred relics.

In the Latin chapel, the altar is the gift of Maximilian of Austria, who later became Emperor of Mexico. Above it is a statue of St. Helena and, on the feast of the Holy Cross (September 13), it is lavishly decorated. The chamber itself gives a good idea of the rock of Calvary and why exactly it got the title "mount." The original reason for the excavation is not clear. It may have been a cistern. It may have been a deep trench connected with the defensive works around Jerusalem and, in particular, with the second wall. It is obvious that Constantine did not fill in the excavation, perhaps because it already had some mysterious religious associations in his time. Only later did the popular beliefs symbolized by St. Helena become attached to it.

As is evident, a cursory study of the geography, history, archaeology and devotion connected with the Holy Sepulcher basilica deepens our appreciation of its meaning. Our Judaeo-Christian religion is not an abstraction devoid of color, movement and location. It is a story of salvation, worked out in human society on this very earth of ours, and our sacred books are filled from beginning to end with geographic specifics. There are sites where God has intervened, and intervened again, to guide human destiny, sometimes paradoxically. The Holy Sepulcher is such a place for Christians. It is full of diversity and of apparent contradictions, but in our own time it has also become a common center of gravity and of unity. Three different Christian communities now collaborate in the preservation of its fabric. Yet, each new column, capital and arch placed in position symbolizes a new-born movement of tolerance, respect, and love, which has opened a new chapter in the story of Jerusalem and of the Christian world at large.

Lutheran Church of the Redeemer, Jerusalem

FROM ONE PARTICULAR spot on the site of the former Jerusalem Temple, one can look over the western skyline and see, framed within a single archway, the tops of shrines belonging to four different faiths. One is the solid tower of the Lutheran church, quite close to the Holy Sepulcher basilica. Where we might expect a building in the stern northern Gothic style, the church is pleasantly Romanesque, resembling something from the warmer climes of Italy or France. The reason for this is the fact that it is really an exact copy of a Crusader church.

The site is ancient. It was formerly the church of St. Mary the Latin, Major, originally a Benedictine foundation and later part of the Hospice of the Knights of St. John. (St. Mary Minor was built later, a hospice for lady pilgrims, staffed by Benedictine nuns.) Sections of the Crusader building are still to be seen, notably the remains of the beautiful chapel, which is now within the residence attached to the church and is entered by a special door to the south. On one side, the delicate arches on the lower floor are supported by three finely worked columns, giving a somewhat Moorish effect, while those of the upper cloister are solidly plain and functional. The medieval doorway is also preserved, simple in itself but decorated with the signs of the zodiac and the symbols of the months.

In 1869, Wilhelm I of Prussia secured title to these ruins from the Sultan, and the present church was built according to the same plan and in the same style as the original. Thus, we have here an excellent illustration of just how the Crusaders constructed their churches in the Holy Land. The typical, solid arches are immediately evident, though the delicate decoration in blue, white and gold gives them an Eastern aspect. The apse is done in gold with a head of the Savior as the central motif. The altar bears a crucifix, and the inscription, in German, reads, "Jesus Christ, yesterday, today, and forever." The pulpit is surmounted by a beautifully carved wooden dome, resembling in shape a flat lantern top, with small Romanesque arches as the constant theme. A bronze inscription on the south wall of the church gives a short history of the building and informs us that the actual construction was carried out in 1893–1898. The Emperor Wilhelm II himself presided over the solemn opening on October 31, 1898. One of the most pleasing features of the furnishings is the fine organ in the left (north) nave. It is used not only for normal liturgical services but also for recitals of sacred music, non-Lutheran artists sometimes being welcomed as performers.

The Erlöser Kirche is the center of the spiritual and social activities of Lutherans in the Holy Land. Lutheranism reaches back here to 1841 when, in common with the Anglican Church, a diocese of Jerusalem was erected. In 1952, all these efforts

116

were coordinated by the foundation of "The Jerusalem Society of Berlin," designed to work in collaboration with the Anglican Church in the southern part of the Holy Land. As a result, there are Arab-Protestant parishes in Beit-Jala, Bethlehem, Beit-Sahur, Ramallah and Jerusalem itself. On July 12, 1959, these came together in synod and erected officially the Lutheran Protestant Church in Jordan.

In the sphere of social activity, the Church educates about eight hundred children in three schools, one of which is a high school. The Schneller Institute runs an orphanage, and the deaconesses of Kaiserswerth teach in the Talitha Kumi secondary school for girls. The Victoria Augusta hospital on the Mount of Olives, a well-known landmark in all Jerusalem, is one of the main centers of Lutheran charitable activity. Protestant pilgrims from all parts of the world join Lutherans in the special ceremonies at Christmas and Holy Week. In the ecumenical sphere, the Lutheran Church is a member of the "Near East Council of Churches," while the present Provost often holds conversations and conferences with visiting German Catholic priests.

Lutheran Church of the Redeemer, Jerusalem.

The Cenacle

It is a great paradox in Christian history that the first Christian church in the world is now quite empty, its form that of a mosque, its guardians Jewish. For centuries, up till the Middle Ages, apparently no great monument marked the spot where the Last Supper was celebrated. Consequently, our modern quest for precision in dating and description is largely baffled here by vague and sometimes contradictory traditions. Yet, the site is rich in Christian memories and, though it is now difficult to become enthusiastic over an abandoned room, some knowledge of its past helps to give it dignity and meaning in our minds and hearts.

The first example of shifting tradition here is the very name of the area in Jerusalem, "Mount Zion." This title was originally given the first Hebrew citadel on the eastern slopes of the modern city site. Gradually, with the expanding population, the name was given to the western hill. With it came Jewish legends, especially the tradition that King David's tomb is to be found on Mount Zion. It is curious that, in his first sermon after Pentecost, St. Peter should note that David's tomb "is with us to this day" (Acts 2:29), for the traditional site of this notable discourse and that of David's tomb itself are nowadays shown in the one building.

So, it is high on the western hill, overlooking the golden city wall and much of Old and New Jerusalem, that we seek out the place where important Christian memories centered. We can be confident that this was the site of a fairly elaborate private home, with a second story and an "upper room" (*hyperoion* in the Greek of Acts 1:13) used by the first followers of Christ, which was big enough to accommodate one hundred and twenty people and was frequented by the first Christians as their own church-synagogue in Jerusalem.

The first recorded event to take place here was a piece of practical business, the election of Matthias as a member of the Twelve in place of Judas (Acts 1:15–26). However, by far the most important event was the coming of the Holy Spirit upon the apostles gathered in this place, changing Synagogue into Church, Jews into Christians, and bringing into being a new kind of Israel (Acts 2). After the Church of the Resurrection, the basilica of the Holy Sepulcher, this house became the most cherished shrine in Christendom. By 130 A.D., there were only a few buildings in the area, one of them being "the little church of God upon the spot. It was build there, that is upon Zion" (Epiphanius). In 348, reference could be made to the "upper" and "lower" churches, the latter being that of the Holy Sepulcher, and the other that higher up on Mount Zion. It was a suitable place for sermons on the Holy Spirit, according to St. Cyril of Jerusalem.

Entrance to the Cenacle, Mount Zion.

The fifth-century pilgrim-nun, Aetheria, loved the liturgy, and she recorded that, on the vigil of Pentecost, the faithful watched through the night in the Church of the Holy Sepulcher. Then, early after Mass, "absolutely everyone accompanies the bishop to Zion, singing hymns on the way, so that by Tierce they are all on Zion. Then they read the passage from the Acts of the Apostles that tells of the descent of the Holy Spirit."

The name of the place in use today, however, makes no reference to the Spirit, but to eating. It is called the Cenacle, or *Cenaculum* (Latin for "dining room" or "refectory"). With the name are associated the most intimate events of Jesus' final days in the company of his disciples: his last celebration of Passover, the washing of his followers' feet, the changing of the Paschal rite into a new worship of thankfulness, the Eucharistic Liturgy, his calm prediction of imminent death, his farewell discourse, and, finally, his appearances after the crucifixion with the promise of great power to the apostles: the faculty to forgive sin. From a further note left by Aetheria, we know that, in her time, the tradition of the resurrection appearances were definitely attached to the church of the Pentecostal happenings. "The passage from the gospels, telling how the Lord came to the disciples through closed doors, is read out on the same day and at the same place, where now the church stands upon Zion."

Curiously, although the Last Supper was eaten in an upper room, the room's exact location is not known to us from early Christian tradition. St. Luke clearly uses two different words in reference to the refectory and the place where the Spirit descended. In Aetheria's time, the institution of the Eucharist was solemnly commemorated yearly, not on Zion but "behind the Cross"—that is, behind Golgotha—emphasizing the close connection between the Cross and the Eucharistic Sacrifice. She tells us that, afterwards, the faithful spent the night on Mount Olivet. Thus, the place of the Last Supper was located by tradition in many different places, even in the Grotto of Gethsemane! In the sixth century, the most constant site of devotion to the Eucharist was the Church of the Resurrection, where a chalice, which was venerated as being the one used at the Last Supper, was displayed.

From this time on, however, there is definite evidence of the association of the Eucharist with Zion. Following a tradition which was already old among them, the Armenians went to Zion and there read an account of the institution of the Eucharist, as written in a Gospel-book dating from 450–500. Only afterwards did they go up to the Mount of Olives for evening prayer. Alexander, a sixth century monk from Cyprus, clearly located the room of the Last Supper on Zion. By the time of the Patriarch Sophronius (d. 638), Zion church was held to be the scene of the great events subsequently associated with it: the coming of the Holy Spirit, the Last Supper, the washing of the feet, the death of Mary.

120

As we see, the written tradition for the Eucharist being celebrated on Zion is vague. However, it is certain that the apostles must first have followed Christ's command, "Do this in memory of me" here, in their own house of prayer. Finally, if we have to choose among all the historical possibilities as to where the Last Supper was actually held, there is no site more logically worthy than that of the present Cenacle.

What has become of the Upper Room today? Given the long history of Jerusalem, we could hardly expect to find the structure still standing in its original state. However, besides venerating the general site and recalling its precious memories, we have good reason to believe that the "Tomb of David" and the "Cenacle" now pointed out to us do really mark the place of the mysteries. This conclusion is based upon a recent close study, conducted especially by Father Bagatti, a Franciscan who has become an expert on Judaeo-Christian monuments. Starting from St. Peter's reference to David's tomb as being "still with us" (Acts 2:29), and from early descriptions of buildings here, he concludes that the present "Tomb of David" really contains remnants of a church-synagogue dating from very early times. This is made clear from a study of four courses of masonry in the southeast corner, of the detail of the apse behind the present cenotaph (dating from medieval times), and especially of Greek inscriptions scratched upon the walls. As deciphered by Father Testa, one of these reads, "O, Jesus! Let me live, O Lord of the sovereign." The "sovereign" referred to is David, as in Psalm 109 (110), the favorite messianic Psalm of early Christians. The name of Jesus is abbreviated to IH, a common primitive Christian symbol, as findings at Nazareth have shown. Another inscription reads, "Conquer, O Savior. Have mercy."

From a study of similar structures in other early churches, we can conclude that, here on Zion, there could have been two sacred monuments within the one building: a church where the Eucharist was celebrated, and a separate, more elaborate place for public assembly, especially for the eating of the common meal, the *agape*. Further excavations beneath the floor of the "Tomb of David" are necessary before all the details can be known. But it is most probable that we still know the location of "the little church of God upon the spot" (Epiphanius) which was later transformed into the fourth-century basilica, called by Theodosius (530) "the mother of all the churches."

Destroyed by the Persians in 614, this church was soon restored by Patriarch Modestus. In time, two important Christian shrines were pointed out here: to the left, a chapel where the Virgin Mary had died; to the right, the Cenacle. Thus, an Armenian document (c. 660) has the interesting note: "To the right of the church is the room of the mysteries and a wooden dome with a painting of the Holy Supper of the Redeemer. It contains an altar where the Liturgy is celebrated." When the Crusaders came, a host of sacred memories already clung to the spot. Known still as the Church of the Holy Spirit, it commemorated the following: the tombs of David, Solomon and Stephen; the death of Mary; the Last Supper; the apparitions after Christ's resurrection; the descent of the Holy Spirit.

The Crusaders soon had a fine new church built on the site, consisting of three naves and a wooden roof. It was known as "St. Mary's of Mount Zion." There was a chapel or edicule commemorating Mary's death, but the Upper Room was kept distinctive. The whole monument was rebuilt in the form of a large dwelling with two floors, each divided down the middle by a row of columns. It has retained this general shape down to our own day. However, the building was pillaged, or fell into ruin, many times.

Between the years 1335 and 1343, the Franciscans were able to buy part of the ruined Crusader basilica. They built a residence and restored the four chapels, the two on the upper floor being dedicated to the memory of the Last Supper and the Holy Spirit, while those below commemorated the tombs of David and St. Francis. This building became the headquarters of the whole Franciscan mission in the Middle East, the Superior being known as, "Guardian of Holy Mount Zion." The presence of Christians on the site of the "Tomb of David," was resented by both Moslems and Jews and, from time to time, the Franciscans lost possession of parts of the monument. They were expelled for good in 1552. Thereupon, Moslem veneration of the tomb of David displaced Christian memories and the place became a center of Islamic worship. Turkish families occupied the former Latin residence, and Christians were forbidden to visit the Sanctuary. In 1831, permission was given them to enter the room of the Cenacle and say some simple prayers, but in 1928, this was turned into a mosque and all public worship on the part of Christians was forbidden once more.

After nearly four hundred years, the Franciscans returned (1936) to within ten meters of the spot, buying a bakery and turning it into a small residence and church *ad Coenaculum*, "By the Cenacle." Behind the altar, a window of clear glass gives a constant view of the lost shrine, allowing the religious to pray and to wait, as they have often successfully done, for the coming of "better times."

In 1948, as so often in military history, the dominant hill of Zion became a battleground in the Arab-Jewish war. The site was occupied by the Israelis, and they have since transformed it into the central religious shrine of their country. The Tomb of David became the focal point of Jewish devotion, while other sections of the Crusader buildings, monuments and relics recall the "Holocaust" of Jews under the Nazi regime. The government of Israel has recently opened up the entire shrine to visitors of all faiths.

Entering the Cenacle today, one passes through the great arches of the Crusader construction, their weight being the more oppressive because the ground level has gradually risen with time. The small cloister is that of a sixteenth-century

The Cenacle.

Franciscan friary. One climbs to the Upper Room by an outside flight of stone steps and enters a completely empty antechamber. Beyond this is the sanctuary. It is in the form of a mosque, but retains the essentials of the Franciscan reconstruction in the fourteenth century: fifteen yards long, nine and a half wide, six and a half high.

Two pillars support the Gothic ceiling and divide the area into two aisles. Three Gothic windows of the fourteenth century give light. Attached to the right-hand wall is a Moslem *mihrab,* or central shrine of worship, while in the corner are the remains of a pulpit with stairs going down to the lower floor. The one slim column of this structure not attached to the wall should be noted. Its Crusader capital bears the rough images of pelicans, with human heads below—symbols of Christ feeding his flock with his own life-giving blood. Arabic inscriptions on the walls dedicate the building to, "Allah, the compassionate, the merciful." An iron railing which used to keep Christians out of the mosque proper is now open and one is permitted private prayers here, but no public worship is allowed.

In the southeast corner, eight steps go up to the little room which is now pointed out as the scene of the events of Pentecost. Standing on this spot, we are reminded of the change of emphasis which has taken place in Christian devotion here. Once, the descent of the Holy Spirit was the focus of attention. Now, the chief room is given over to commemoration of the Last Supper. To the Western mind, it is a little puzzling, but to Orientals it is quite logical. It is the meaning of the central mysteries which matters. It is this reality which has been carried throughout the world from Zion, the mother and head of all the churches, by the same Spirit who both spoke through the words of the Eucharistic discourse at the Last Supper and who, so soon after, came down as the apostolic Spirit of Pentecost.

Basilica of the Agony, Gethsemane

THE MYSTERIES OF Christ's suffering and death are commemorated chiefly in the basilica of the Holy Sepulcher. The further mystery of his full acceptance of this foreknown ordeal is associated, in Christian tradition, with the valley to the east of Jerusalem, outside the walls. Today, as one looks across from the older part of the city, one sees something on the hillside which is comparatively rare here: trees, olive trees. It was in a garden at the foot of this Mount of Olives that Christ prayed to be spared from the trial of torture and death, and where, finally, among the trees, he consented to it all, thus making his passion, literally, the supreme sacrifice. The place is still known as Geth-semane (from the Hebrew term for "oil press"), and a majestic basilica, together with a lowly grotto-chapel, mark the site of Christ's Agony.

Basilica of the Agony, Gethsemane, Kidron Valley, Jerusalem.

The task of building and adorning the modern basilica posed a fundamental challenge to Christian art. The theme is so filled with mystery that it could never have been adequately expressed in some obvious or realistic style. The representation had to be essentially abstract, yet impressive and edifying, evoking a sincere response in the mind and heart of the beholder, setting his inspiration free. Artists intimately acquainted with the mysteries themselves were needed, and, providentially, they were found.

Antonio Barluzzi was the architect, he who marked the Holy Land with its finest churches. On Mount Tabor, he used to the full the element of light. In Gethsemane, he dimmed light almost to the point of obscurity, to bring to mind the near-night of the soul which Christ entered here. Some think the building too dark, but a right approach helps us appreciate the architecture which is really something quite unique.

It is a mistake to enter by the main doors, which are left open. For one thing, the façade is cut off too abruptly by the main road for a suitable approach to the whole monument. For about ten minutes inside, the eyes will see almost nothing of the detail. The strong, natural light from outside will destroy the essential, somber atmosphere of the interior. But if the visitor goes in by the side entrance, he will first walk through the garden and establish right away the familiar motif here: eight hoary olive trees, still productive, the fruit yielding oil, the stones being used to fashion rosary beads to be sent out from Jerusalem to all quarters of the globe.

Passing through the sacristy, you immediately see the main feature of the whole shrine: the large, bare, sandstone rock in front of the altar, traditionally the stone on which Christ prayed during his agony. Light from above focuses attention on it. Gradually, other elements in the decoration of the church become clear. The first is the great iron wreath, in the shape of a crown of thorns, which surrounds the rock and which is expressive of the suffering of mind and heart undergone by Christ. His innocence and helplessness is symbolized by a white dove caught in the spikes and slowly dying in agony. The bitterness of his experience is again brought out through the symbolism of two birds, one standing on each side of a plain chalice. Their look of startled dismay on sipping the contents of the cup is quite wonderfully portrayed.

After the rock, the large mosaic above the altar should be contemplated, for it graphically interprets the central story of Gethsemane. High above, in the first register, the hand of God the Father appears, bearing the wreath of eventual victory, the assurance that Christ is not wholly abandoned. In the middle, the comforting angel comes down. Finally, in the main mosaic, Christ is shown leaning against the rock, the face strained with deep fatigue, with puzzlement and bewilderment, perhaps, but still quite calm. This masterpiece, by D'Achiardi, sets the high standard of adornment through the whole church. It has been described by an expert, Dominican Father Vincent, as "a marvel of art and of lofty religious inspiration. Two great olive trees frame the central figure of Christ, while the three weary disciples sleep beside one of the gnarled trunks. This painting in small mosaic stones has a vocabulary of its own which no other medium can really rival. Its lasting power to impress is quite superlatively employed in the basilica of the Agony.

Turning to the body of the church, we see how, in detail, the architect has ingeniously created the atmosphere of the central mystery. Six monolithic columns support the ceiling, which is in the form of little domes adorned with olive branches and the stars of a clear night sky. Through the alabaster windows, translucent but not transparent, filters a violet light, the liturgical color for mourning and penance. Other mosaics bring out the great paradoxes of the story of the Agony at its end: that of the kiss of Judas, and that of Christ's majestic declaration, *Ego sum,* "I am," with attendants falling to the ground before the claim to divinity implicit in these words, understood according to the overtones of the Fourth Gospel (John 18:6; Exodus 3:14). The main altar with its somber color, shot through with veins of red, is in itself a symbol of the bloody sweat of Christ in this place, while the side altars, though necessarily of small dimensions, are not wanting in elegance and strength.

The coats of arms of many countries appear on the ceiling and in the mosaics, reminding us that the church was built through the worldwide generosity of Christians. For this reason, it is often called "The Church of all Nations." (One naturally seeks mention of one's own homeland and, at first, the author thought that his had been forgotten once again. But a closer study of the iron wreath around the very rock itself in front of the altar revealed a discreet inscription in Latin: "Gerardi fashioned it; Australia gave it.")

As so often happens, the floor of the basilica is a reminder of the long tradition which lies behind the shrine. As will be noted, clear evidence of a fourth-century church on this site came to light during preparatory excavations for the modern building. These remains can be seen by removing the mats which cover the present church floor.

Coming at last to the main entrance outside, we can study some of the magnificent detail of the façade. In sight of Jerusalem's Golden Gate and of the dome of the mosque of Omar on the site of the ancient Jewish Temple, the theme here is that of the acceptance by God of Christ's supreme sacrifice. In other words, the priesthood of Christ is celebrated majestically. The Latin text below the great triangle *(tympanum)* reads, "[Jesus] offered up prayers and supplications, with loud cries and tears, and he was heard for his godly fear" (Hebrews 5:7). The large mosaic shows various members of the human race, working and suffering,

128

surrounding a sympathetic Christ and placing their trust in him. Above, a cross crowns all, but it is flanked by two stags symbolizing the words of Psalm 42:1 (words of confidence amidst near despair): "As a hart longs for flowing streams, so longs my soul for thee, O God." Statues of the four evangelists stand above the magnificent capitals which crown the multiple supporting columns of the façade. The ironwork of the surrounding fences is gracefully wrought, showing in some panels the fish-scale motif common in early Christian churches. During the day, with the sun behind, it throws a pleasant pattern onto the nearby pavement.

The antiquity of the site and the continuity of tradition here has been demonstrated in modern times by careful excavation. In 1891 and 1901, the remains of a Crusader church called St. Savior's were found. However, it was in 1920, when the deeper foundations of the modern basilica were being prepared, that the relics of a much older building were revealed in great detail. This is undoubtedly the Byzantine church which Aetheria visited and described as "elegant." The archaeologists brought to light clear traces of three aisles, a sample of a fine capital, and parts of a rich mosaic floor as well as mural decorations. Most interesting were the traces of the foyer or atrium with its cistern intact. Direct contact with this ancient tradition is evident in the modern church floor where the design of the old pavement is closely followed and the water-motif is expressed in white and green marble.

Because it was built outside the walls of Jerusalem, the Byzantine church was one of the first to be destroyed by the Persians in 614. Top-soil gradually covered the sacred rock, but Christians continued to bury their dead nearby, thus prolonging the age-old memories and helping to preserve it from further destruction.

The Grotto of the Agony

CLOSE BY THE basilica to the north is a large cave of irregular shape, 17 meters long and 9 wide, rising to a maximum of 3.50 high. This grotto would often have sheltered Jesus and his disciples when, "as was his custom," he went to Gethsemane (Luke 22:39–40; Matthew 26:36). Here, Christian memory associated with Christ's Passion that of his betrayal by his follower, Judas "who also knew the place; for Jesus often met there with his disciples" (John 18:2–6). Only after the ancient churches of the Agony had been destroyed were liturgical ceremonies transferred to the cave, and the concept of the Agony itself displaced that of the betrayal— hence, the present name.

In the twelfth century, the cave was richly adorned with mosaics but, with time, these largely disappeared and it came to resemble closely the form it had in Christ's own day. However, in 1959, it was restored and given a somewhat more

regular appearance. The entrance was widened and reshaped, and above it quotations from the Gospel passages of the Passion, referred to already, were placed. A floor and three altars have been provided, together with appropriate frescoes above each: over the main altar, Jesus praying with his apostles; over the left altar, the Assumption of Mary; over the one on the right, the Kiss of Judas.

Here, modern archaeology has once again confirmed tradition, especially on this site of the Grotto of the Agony. In 1956, a thorough examination of the place was undertaken. Clear evidence came to light that, in the time of Jesus and his first followers, there was truly an agricultural establishment here, and in the precise form of an olive press. Traces of the apparatus of the press itself, together with those of a water catchment system, exclude the idea that the cave was originally used as a cemetery. They support the Gospel tradition that it could have frequently provided a refuge for Jesus and his disciples in the Kidron valley, within sight of the walls of Jerusalem.

Subsequent excavations showed how the grotto was transformed into a church. At the beginning of the fourth century, the sanctuary was fashioned over the site of the press itself, being separated from the main body of the chapel by an altar railing. Then, the rich mosaic floor began, many samples of which have come to light. In the Byzantine period (5th and 6th centuries), it became customary to bury Christians beneath the floor; and from that time onward the mosaic suffered greatly, more than forty separate graves having been dug. Fragmentary remains of inscriptions have been found, one with the liturgical formula, "Lord, grant rest...," but the proper name of the deceased is missing.

Of the Crusader restoration of the grotto, not a great deal was revealed. Star designs were used in the decoration of the ceiling and mosaics in the floor. In post-Crusader times, the grotto became a burial place once more.

Every year on Holy Thursday, a ceremonial watch of one hour is held in the basilica in memory of Christ's Agony in Gethsemane. At this time we are intimately drawn into contact with the mystery by the inspired architecture and artistry of a great church. We are further stimulated by the thought that the story we relive has surely remained vivid here through hundreds of years, back to the time of the apostles themselves.

Christ in prayer, Grotto of the Agony, Gethsemane.

Monastery of the Cross, Jerusalem

JERUSALEM IS A city of great contrasts, particularly the prosperous, modern sector to the west. Here, for example, you find recent architecture at its best in the new Knesset (Parliament), the University halls and the Museum. All of these immediately overlook a valley which is almost untamed, with gnarled olive trees growing amongst white stone outcrops in the hot, still air. One ancient building, massive and grey, stands at the bottom of the gulley. It is the Monastery of the Cross, which has given its name to the area, *Wadi el-Musallabe* ("Valley of the Cross") and has centuries of interesting history behind it. Unlike so many other monuments here, it was destroyed only once, by the Persians, though it has often been pillaged and restored.

Entering by a very low door, we find an inner court surrounded by heavily buttressed walls, which rest, possibly, on Roman foundations. The silver dome and belfry alone suggest from outside that the building was once a Crusader shrine. Around and above the court are the military-like arrangement of stairways and terraces which provided living quarters built onto the walls. From the court, a narrow passage leads to the church which is the main feature of the building. It has kept its Crusader character with the usual, beautifully vaulted ceilings and a high dome above the altar. One item of interest is the mosaic floor showing designs of animals and fashioned according to Byzantine models of the fifth or sixth centuries, though actually placed in position much later. By far the most interesting features of this church are the many frescoes and designs on the walls and pillars, with quite an unusual theme.

Christian piety, particularly in the Middle Ages, sought the origin of many religious practices in antiquity, especially in the Bible. Two legends came into being, explaining the remote reasons for venerating the cross of Christ and the expiation made thereon. One goes back to the biblical father of us all, Adam. About to die, Adam asked for a twig from the Tree of Knowledge, placed it in his mouth and expired. His relatives tried to remove it, but in vain. He was buried with the twig, which eventually took root and grew into a tree, imprisoning the skull of Adam in its fabric. From this tree the cross of Christ was ultimately fashioned, and thus the first drops of his redeeming blood fell on the head of our common father. This legend, perpetuated also in the chapel of Adam under Calvary, is portrayed by the skull sometimes attached to crucifixes beneath Christ's feet.

The other story of the origin of the cross begins with a later biblical personality, Lot. Remorse for his sins of incest (Genesis 19:36) drove the Patriarch to look for a sign from God that his guilt had been pardoned. An angel appeared and gave him three cypress twigs. These were to be planted and watered daily, but with water brought from afar, from the Jordan river. If the twigs struck root, Lot was to know that he was forgiven. Lot did as he was directed and the shoots began to grow. However, on one occasion as the Patriarch was returning from the river, a demon appeared in the form of a beggar and asked for water. Despite his anxiety for the newly-struck plant, Lot complied. When the demon proceeded to drink the whole supply of water, Lot's uneasiness turned to fear. However, the angel appeared once more and assured him that his act of charity was most pleasing to God, that the cypress would continue to grow and that his sins had been forgiven. Ultimately, the full grown tree was cut for timber for Solomon's Temple, but was not used. It was left lying to serve as a bench for visitors. It was from this tree trunk that the cross of Christ was ultimately made.

Such stories will hardly bear the surgery of modern historical criticism—nor were they ever intended to do so. They represent a simple, devout mentality which constantly sought to renew its spirituality in concrete forms, particularly through reference to the whole Judaeo-Christian history of salvation. These legends have edified thousands in the past, one proof of this being the fact that the finest frescoes in the Monastery of the Cross repeat in serial fashion the narrative of Lot's tree. Thus, we are shown Lot receiving the three twigs from Abraham. Another picture represents Lot watering the tree with its triple branches, now grown taller than himself. A third fresco depicts a weary Lot returning with skin water-bottles on an ass, the horned demon stalking in the background. Towards the end of the series, two men bearing the horizontal beam of the cross, finally fashioned from the famous tree, are shown. Lastly, Christ is pictured being nailed to this cross in sight of Roman soldiers and the faithful womenfolk. Other paintings refer to biblical themes associated with the legends. One has Abraham receiving the three distinguished guests who foretell the birth of Isaac (Genesis 18:1–15). In the background his wife, Sarah, laughs at the whole idea, sheltering under the famous oak tree of Mamre. Another fresco shows Lot escaping from Sodom with his two daughters while, behind, his wife lingers curiously and is slowly changed into a statue of salt (Genesis 19:18–29). The clearest of these pictures are to be found on the walls at the back of the altar. Here also is pointed out the exact spot where the tree of the legend grew.

The long history of the monastery is a reminder to Western visitors of the many nationalities who, in the past, have contributed to the religious history of Palestine. In this case, there is question of folk from Georgia (now a republic of the Soviet Union) who, together with the Armenians, brought deep faith and a constant devotion to the Holy Land from the Caucasus.

The Georgians have been Christians from very early times and they consider the apostle St. Andrew to have been their religious founder. One of the principal royal dynasties of Georgia even claimed to have its origins in David. Georgian pilgrims were frequent visitors to Jerusalem, while their religious were established at a shrine most intimately connected with the Cross: Golgotha. It was but logical that, as their influence grew, they should try to set up their headquarters in a monastery built on the site of the very origin of the cross. Eventually, they did get possession of this ancient building in a Jerusalem valley and, from the Middle Ages to the end of the 17th century, it was the center of Georgian religious and cultural activity in the Holy Land.

The actual foundation of the Monastery of the Cross is attributed to various royal personages, but it is likely that the Byzantine conqueror of the Persians, Emperor Heraclius, on his visit to Jerusalem (c. 630) had the foundation begun, possibly on earlier Roman remains. Between 1038 and 1057, a Georgian monk, Prokhoré, rebuilt the church and monastery, supported by the Georgian royal family of the time. The Crusaders left the eastern monks in possession and, thanks to a skilful policy of neutrality on the part of their kings, the position of the Georgians actually improved when Saladin took Jerusalem from the Crusaders in 1187. They were quick to obtain rights and titles which they held until the seventeenth century, expanding their religious and cultural influence throughout the whole of Palestine. In the 14th and 15th centuries, the Georgians were easily the most important religious organization in the Holy Land, occupying many of the most significant Orthodox monasteries, with the Monastery of the Cross as their headquarters. However, at the end of the 15th century, their influence began to decline and they had to withdraw religious gradually from many of their former houses. It was precisely in these circumstances that, in 1560, the Franciscans were able to acquire the Monastery of Saint Savior, Jerusalem. It has remained the headquarters of the Franciscan Custody of the Holy Land ever since.

Finally, the Monastery of the Cross remained the sole Georgian possession in all Palestine and, despite a generous effort to revive it in 1643, the financial situation of the community became hopeless. The establishment was taken over by the Greek Orthodox Church and has since remained in their hands, the building being used at times as a theological seminary. Religious services are still held in the beautiful church. The cultural contribution which the monastery made for many centuries is still represented by a great, rich mass of manuscripts, illuminations and documents kept in the library of the Greek Orthodox Patriarchate, Jerusalem.

Russian Church of the Ascension, Jerusalem

APPROACHING JERUSALEM FROM Jericho and the south, the first unmistakable landmark seen is a slim, soaring church-tower reaching for the skies on Mount Olivet. It is the "Russian Candle of the Holy Land" marking their Church of the Ascension—a lasting monument to a deep Christian faith which, in the past, generously adorned Palestine with Russian foundations.

Indicative of the present parlous economic position in which the Russian Christian community now finds itself is the fact that the church and its tower are at present closed, due to the urgent need for repairs. Formerly, with its six stories and 214 steps, the latter gave a glorious view of all Judaea and the surrounding countryside. Yet, it was not built merely for show. It had a practical purpose, linked to the main mission of Russian foundations here: the reception and guidance of pilgrims who were never mere tourists, but made their visit from far-off Russia a genuine religious experience. The tower served elderly folk who could not possibly make the journey to the Jordan, affording them a distant glimpse of the place where Christ was baptized in the river waters.

The grounds of the compound are beautifully wooded and, as we pass through, we feel already something of the peaceful atmosphere in which the Sisters pass their days. They have been here since the area was handed over to them in 1907. The church itself, built in 1881, is not pretentious, but is heavily adorned with paintings done by the nuns, most being representations of the motherhood of Mary. At the southeast corner of the building, there is a stone which reputedly marks the place where Christ's mother, Mary, stood at the time of the Ascension. The great bell in the tower was transported here by Russian womenfolk all the way from Jaffa on the coast, since the Moslem workmen had certain misgivings about erecting bells.

To the east of the main church is another smaller one, built on an ancient site. It is dedicated to St. John the Baptist. The central feature here is a rich mosaic which marks the site of an Armenian tomb but which actually was inserted into a much older design dating from the 5th or 6th century. There is a hole here, and an ancient document on the wall states that it was on this spot that the head of St. John the Baptist was found. Hence, the name of this second church, dedicated to the Baptist. An Armenian writer of the 7th century mentions two Armenian Convents on Olivet, one sacred to St. John the Precursor. We may be confident that the present church bearing his name marks the site.

The life of the Sisters resembles closely that of Latin enclosed nuns. They make profession of the rule of St. Basil the Great, with the customary three vows of poverty, chastity, and obedience. However, these are of an especially solemn

form which permits the Sisters to receive Holy Communion weekly, instead of monthly as is usual in the Orthodox Church. Arab girls apply for admission as novices, and this keeps up the numbers in the community which, of course, gets no recruits from modern Russia. The Sisters maintain themselves by manual labor, especially by fashioning beautiful church vestments, miters, copes and stoles. Another source of support is the generosity of Americans of Russian origin, among whom, in New York, is the Metropolitan, the leader of all Russian Christians outside the homeland. The Sisters are acutely aware of the need to promote the ecumenical movement towards the union of all Christians, yet they are frank in stating the difficulties from their point of view. Perhaps, their devotion to the Holy Spirit and to the Heart of Christ will help solve these eventually and bring the great community of Russian Orthodoxy into the universal Christian union.

Church of the Dormition, Jerusalem

THE CHRISTIAN GOSPELS make rare mention of Mary, the mother of Jesus. There is some detail about the early years of her motherhood and several notices concerning three episodes during Christ's public life and Passion, but about her own death there is nothing at all. Yet, Christian devotion began very early to meditate on her career, with its unusual end, and there developed a great wealth of legend concerning it. Some of this has been recorded, the literature being grouped by scholars under the general title, *Transitus Mariae,* "The Passing of Mary." But, there is little in it to satisfy our modern, more prosaic search for actual historical detail.

It is the Acts of the Apostles in the New Testament which provides the earliest and most genuine indication of Mary's way of life after Jesus had gone: "All these [the apostles] with one accord devoted themselves to prayer, together with the women and Mary the mother of Jesus, and with his brothers" (Acts 1:14). The place would have been the "Upper Room" on what is now called Mount Zion, Jerusalem. It is here that a long tradition has firmly located the scene of Mary's passing.

Nothing is known about early Christian veneration of Mary on this spot, possibly because it was for some three hundred years exclusively the center of Judaeo-Christian worship, avoided by people of Gentile origin and especially by Westerners. However, when the original little church, built on the site of the Cenacle, was included in the Byzantine basilica erected by Bishop John of Jerusalem (386–417), the memory of Mary's death was also attached, and this later became localized in one special place. So, in the early 7th century, a Patriarch-poet of Jerusalem, Sophronius, could commemorate both Mary's spiritual motherhood

and, in more detail, the stone in the basilica on which this "daughter of God" had expired. About the middle of the same century, a Western visitor, Arculf, could draw a plan of the church showing the place where Mary had died.

In the time of the Crusades, the memory of Mary prevailed over that of all others associated with the Mother of all the Churches on Zion. The medieval basilica was named quite simply "St. Mary's on Mount Zion." John of Würzburg (1165) describes how the building housed a special chapel commemorating Mary's death. It was wholly adorned with marble, enclosed by a wrought-iron railing and surmounted by a canopy bearing the words "The holy Mother of God is borne up above the choirs of the angels." On the wall, there was a picture of Jesus, surrounded by the apostles, receiving her soul.

From the time when the Franciscans acquired the site of the Cenacle (1335/1337), and through the long subsequent story of usurpation and expulsion, they kept the memory of Mary alive on Zion. It was because they had built an oratory dedicated to the Virgin that they were forced to hand over all the shrines here to the Moslems on May 23, 1490. Throughout the following centuries, however, pilgrims were still directed to the traditional place of Mary's passing, called by the Moslems *Niyaha* ("Lamentation for the dead") and by Christians, *Dormitio* or *Kaimesis* ("The Falling Asleep").

In 1898, the Sultan Abdul Hamid gave the Niyaha garden to Emperor Wilhelm II of Germany, and the history of the great modern basilica and monastery of the Dormition began. The site became the property of the Catholic See of Cologne, and, on October 7, 1900, the foundation stone of the church was laid. On March 21, 1906, after much negotiation, it was entrusted to the German Benedictines of Beuron. In 1951, the Abbey became independent, subject immediately to Rome. The Abbot exercises jurisdiction also over Weston Priory, Vermont, in the United States of America, and monks from here also serve the Church of the Multiplication of Bread, Tabgha, Galilee.

The Cologne architect, Renard, designed the neo-Romanesque church in imitation of Charlemagne's famous Palace Chapel at Aix-la-Chapelle. The classical, octagonal style of mausoleum influenced the planning of the interior. Another, much more ancient example of this is found close by in the Holy Land, in the form of "Absalom's Tomb," Kidron Valley, Jerusalem. The German structure is quite massive, reminding us of castles in northern Europe, and is easily the outstanding landmark in western Jerusalem. However, it is in the decoration of the building that true Christian art is found. It could never be mistaken for anything else, and is a credit to the Benedictine tradition which has both restored the Liturgy to the Latin Church and opened a new era in Catholic artistry.

The upper church is quite functional, the altar being the focal point. It bears an image of the Lamb, in mosaic. Behind it is the monastic choir, and, above this, right across the whole domed apse, is a majestic mosaic of Mary and Child, the Greek abbreviations standing for, "Mary" and "Son of God." Christ holds a book open at the reading (in Greek): "I am the light of the world." In front of the altar, the marble floor bears an inscription, *Lauda Sion Salvatorem,* "Zion, praise the Savior." The remainder of the church floor is one glorious concentric design in color and lettering. In the middle of the design is the symbol of the Trinity, with the *Trisagion* in Greek: "Holy, Holy, Holy," with appropriate quotations in Latin from the Athanasian Creed. The second circle bears the names of the Old Testament personalities who, above all others, brought God to men: the prophets. In the outer circle are the names of the prophets of the New Testament, the apostles.

The side altars in this upper church celebrate devotion to Mary, mother of men in both East and West. The first (going clockwise) is dedicated to the Virgin as the Daughter of her People, *Regina Orientis sis Lumen Gentis* ("Queen of the East, be a light to the People"). The second and third altars commemorate Mary as Queen of Pilgrims and Queen of Monks, with appropriate decoration, especially from Benedictine history. The fourth altar is sacred to Mary, Queen of the West, with the simple prayer: "Queen of the West, save us!" The fifth and sixth shrines are dedicated to "Queen of Prophets," and "Queen of Patriarchs," respectively. They are richly adorned with Old Testament figures in mosaic.

Below the main church is the crypt with its own special motif. The central shrine is in the form of an octagon of pillars, surrounded by a railing and supporting a canopy. Within lies the almost life-sized and delicately fashioned statue of Mary in a brown shroud, asleep in death. The inside of the dome bears mosaic pictures of famous women in the Bible story: Ruth, Judith, and others. Softly illumined by controlled light—for instance, on a winter's evening—the whole sanctuary is most impressive.

In the background, there glows an altar dedicated to the twelve apostles, in whose company Mary had often prayed, and some of whom must have been with her when she died. The side altars around the mausoleum commemorate various mysteries of the Rosary, the paintings being done in a graphic, modern style.

Thus, the memory of Mary's passing from this world is fittingly venerated. The great mass of the Benedictine dome and tower, church and abbey, provoke interest in it still. Devotion is enkindled by the beautiful interior, a religious masterpiece amongst the very finest in the Middle East. The whole monument continues to mark a historic site, that of Zion, of the Mother of all the Churches, the house of prayer to which Mary remained attached until the day she passed from this world.

The Tomb of the Virgin

JEWISH FOLK AS a rule, would never bury their dead within the city walls. Consequently, on the outskirts of Jerusalem, thousands of graves are to be found, especially in the Kidron Valley and up the slopes of the Mount of Olives. It was in this area, too, that tradition located the temporary resting place of Mary in death, quite close to the Grotto of Gethsemane. Because of the age-old belief that Mary's body did not remain in the grave, the monument has the double title, "The Tomb of the Virgin" and "Church of the Assumption." An ornamented Crusader doorway is the only remarkable feature of the shrine which is in the form of a crypt, deep beneath the modern ground level.

Clear evidence of the belief that Mary was buried here goes back at least to the middle of the 4th century, for we know that a small church stood on the site in the time of Theodosius the Great (379–395). There followed a Byzantine basilica, constructed by Patriarch Juvenal of Jerusalem (451–458). This was known as St. Mary's Basilica, or, The Church of our Lady Mary. Destroyed by the Persians in 614, it was soon rebuilt and the pilgrim Arculf (670), who had an excellent eye for detail, tells us that, "The monument consists of two churches, one above the other, round in shape and resting on foundations of quite rare stones. To the east there is an altar and, to the right of this, the marble sepulcher which once held the body of the Virgin Mary." Destroyed by Hakim in the eleventh century, the building was magnificently restored by the Crusaders.

The plan they followed was that described by Arculf. In addition to the architecture, elegance was added in the form of paintings on the walls showing scenes of the death, burial and assumption of Mary. Beside the basilica, the Crusaders erected a monastery for the Benedictines of Cluny. They served in the church, took care of visitors, engaged in farming and, above all, so spread the Benedictine ideal in the Holy Land that this foundation became the source of widespread cultural activity in East and West. Many notables were buried in the church, including Queen Millicent, daughter of Baldwin II.

The monastery and basilica were destroyed in 1187 but, because of Moslem veneration of *Sitti Mariam,* Lady Mary, the crypt was left intact. The Franciscans gained possession in 1392 and often saved it from ruin in the floods which were frequent in this low-lying area. In 1757 they lost control of the shrine to the Greek Orthodox, and, though they visit officially once a year, they hold no public services within.

The nearest monument to Catholic devotion to the mystery is the altar of the Assumption in the nearby Grotto of Gethsemane. Entering by the Crusader door, we see immediately the long flight of 45 steps downward. At the bottom, doors

141

on the north and west sides open into the burial chamber. We are reminded of the Holy Sepulcher in Jerusalem, for an identical procedure was followed by the architects of this shrine: the surrounding rock was removed and even the ante-chamber or vestibule customary in Jewish tombs disappeared. The actual ledge where the body lay is covered by a marble slab, and rich decorations in the Greek style—tapestry, lamps and candles—are abundant. An icon shows Mary's body surrounded by the apostles, while, in the background, Christ holds in his arms a small object, the soul of Mary about to be taken to heaven. To the right of the tomb is a *mihrab* or Moslem shrine, where people of a non-Christian religion sometimes pray. The altar opposite the tomb belongs to the Orthodox Armenians, as also the one near the wall of the tomb. Besides these religious bodies, the Syrians, Copts and Abyssinians (all Orthodox) have certain rights here.

Going back up the stairs, one finds a chapel on the left dedicated to Sts. Joachim and Anne, the parents of Mary. Queen Millicent's remains were deposited here in 1161. Opposite is the chapel of St. Joseph, where other royal personalities were buried. Behind the altar is a long chamber with a tomb at the end, and it is possible that other notables of the Crusader period were laid to rest here. Noteworthy are the marks on the walls left by the medieval stone masons.

Leaving the shrine, one can admire the detail of the Crusader door. Beneath the courtyard, the remains of a large water-catchment in the form of a cistern were found, the supporting pillars numbering 143. Remains of the Benedictine monastery have been discovered nearby, as also in the Franciscan property across the road.

Tomb of the Virgin, Gethsemane.

Church of St. Lazarus, Bethany

ONE PECULIARITY IN the story of Jesus is that, so far as we know, he never spent a night in the city of Jerusalem. In the Kidron valley below the Mount of Olives, within sight of the Temple, he had a favorite retreat for prayer. His regular lodging place, however, was over the mountain and eastward on the Jericho side, in a small village called Bethany. Here he found a true home. Here, even more than in Nazareth, we know how warmly he was received within a family circle. And here, not surprisingly, he proclaimed to dear friends some of the deepest truths of all his teaching.

For many centuries, the exact site of Bethany was unknown. Guides made vague mention of the town, situating it somewhere beyond Mount Olivet. It was not until the Franciscans undertook archaeological excavations, in 1949, that the history of the place was resurrected. This patient and expert labor, directed and reported by Fathers Saller and Bagatti, remains one of the best examples of such careful excavation in all Palestine.

In 1952–1953, the site of the Gospel narratives was crowned by a beautiful church, another masterpiece produced by the versatile genius of architect Antonio Barluzzi. As often happened during his long career of building in the Holy Land, Barluzzi was faced with the dual task of erecting a suitable monument to the particular mysteries commemorated while respecting their historical context by preserving the remains of traditional veneration there. In Bethany, such vestiges were particularly elaborate, previous monuments comprising four successive churches and a large monastery. A study of the detail of these helps us to appreciate centuries of devotion to Jesus who here graciously revealed himself as friend, master, and lord.

The very nature of the memories associated with Bethany create a tension for anyone committed to commemorating them permanently. Here are recalled the close friendship of Jesus with Lazarus and his sisters, Martha and Mary; the promise of eternal resurrection made to Martha; the raising of Lazarus from the grave, and the feast in the home of Simon where Mary anointed Jesus. A little to the west is shown the actual tomb where Lazarus had been laid to rest. Thus, these memories converge in sharp contrast: one facet is dark and somber, as of the tomb; the other is irridescent, hopefully bespeaking resurrection from the grave. As light and shade are used in visual art, so the architect of this church utilized the same contrast to bring out the joy of survival over and above the sadness of death. In this sense, Antonio Barluzzi here combined in one monument what he had done at Tabor, with its wonderfully sun-lit basilica, and with what he achieved in the basilica of Gethsemane, where he dimmed light by use of the violet

shades of mourning. Moreover, he was limited by the existing elements of the site, in the sense that he had to respect the relics of former buildings by allowing them to contribute to the venerable traditions commemorated, and by leaving them open to the view of faithful Christians, scholars, and other visitors.

The modern church is really quite small. It has the form of a Greek cross, with an internal length of 17.70 meters, and a square under the cupola measuring 7.70 meters on each side. The building is isolated from its immediate surroundings, except for the sacristy which joins it to the nearby religious residence. Its walls are almost hermetically sealed and windowless. The dome is solidly incorporated into the octagonal drum overhead. All this suggests a subterranean vault, lonely as a grave. However, as we shall see, this architectural simplicity is relieved by the nobility of the materials used and by the fine sculpture and mosaic decoration.

Coming up the drive from the main road, the visitor will be able to study the church from many points of view. The northeast corner is marked by a slim, unadorned tower, austere as an obelisk. Passing around to the façade (west side), we see that, as in the case of the other three end-walls, it is divided into three panels. It is built of hard stone from the Bethlehem area and dressed in two different degrees of fineness. The bronze door has six panels, each containing a circle surrounded by endless tresses, symbolic of immortality. Above, three mosaic panels represent the saintly persons associated with the site: in the center, Lazarus, the patron of the church; then his sisters, Martha and Mary, on each side. Over this, in turn, there is a sculptured cross which serves also the practical purpose of allowing air to circulate in the interior. Otherwise, the main entrance is quite plain. The eastern wall overlooking the Jerusalem-Jericho road is similarly decorated by three mosaic panels, showing Lazarus in the center flanked by two angels with trumpets, recalling his resurrection from the dead. The other two outside walls have no decoration at all.

Inside the building, the eye is struck by the three dimensions of the decorated floor, the highly ornamented walls, and the opening at the top of the dome which is the sole source of light. The extremities of the cross-shaped building are also seen, and we are given a pleasant impression of generous dimensions, over and above the actual size. The walls of bare polished grey stone are crowned by a horizontal band with inscriptions, and this, in turn, forms the base of the barrel vaults at the end of each arm of the church. The four main arches springing from the piers of the central square are united by smaller spherical ones, which effect the transition from the square to the circle of the dome. At the base of the cupola, variety is introduced by the mosaic inscription on a golden background. The arches are of a yellowish, ivory-like stone from Bethlehem, while the ribbing and panels of the dome are all adorned with mosaic. Thus, the upper part of the building is resplendent with light, while the vaults are shaded. We can see how the architect used simplicity of line, plainly colored stone and reduced height, to create a sense of severity and somberness in the lower half of the church, while the soaring, higher elements, crowned by the dome with its flood of light, suggests the joy of intense hope and optimism. The detail of the decoration bears out this dual theme.

Directly opposite the entrance is the main altar. On its front there are two small pilasters of Bethlehemite stone and, between them, a sculptured slab showing two angelic figures drawing aside a curtain to reveal an empty tomb and a folded shroud. This recalls the grave which Lazarus left. The reredos behind the altar is of desert stone of a red-violet color, with brown and green spots, producing a fine, natural effect. The other two altars, at the end of the north and south arms of the building, are in the form of a sarcophagus or stone coffin, reminding us once more of the basic theme of the sanctuary. Their only ornamentation is a small circular medallion in front, showing figures of Martha and Mary.

The decoration of the semicircular areas above the altars spells out the symbolism below. Over the main altar, a mosaic shows Jesus, with all the majesty of his being, addressing Martha, Mary, and friends: "I am the resurrection and life." These words, and others which complete the story of Lazarus' resurrection (John 11:17–44), are written in Latin along the lateral walls. Over the side-altar to the left (north), we are shown Jesus in the intimacy of the family circle instructing Martha in the paradoxical priorities implied by friendship with Christ. The inscriptions remind us of the main texts: "Lord, do you not care that my sister has left me to serve alone? Tell her then to help me. But the Lord answered her, Martha, Martha, you are anxious and troubled about many things; one thing is needful. Mary has chosen the good portion, which shall not be taken away from her" (Luke 10:40–42).

Above the side-altar to the right (south), we see Jesus raising Lazarus from the grave, in the presence of his sisters, the apostles, the Virgin Mary, and friends. The text below explains the picture: "Then Jesus, deeply moved again, came to the tomb; . . . So they took away the stone. And Jesus lifted up his eyes and said, 'Father, I thank thee that thou hast heard me'. . . When he had said this, he cried out with a loud voice, 'Lazarus, come out.' The dead man came out, his hands and feet wrapped with a cloth. Jesus said to them, 'Unbind him, and let him go.'" (John 11:38–44)

Finally, on the entrance wall over the door there is a picture of the supper in the home of Simon, with Mary anointing Jesus. Again, a seeming paradox is supported by Christ, as the words of the text remind us: "And while he was at Bethany in the house of Simon the leper, as he sat at table, a woman came with an alabaster jar of ointment of pure nard, very costly, and she broke the jar and poured it over his head. . . . But Jesus said, 'Let her alone; why do you trouble her? . . . She had done what she could; she has anointed my body beforehand for burying'" (Mark 14:3–8).

At the base of the dome, the circular cornice carries these words against a golden background: "He who believes in me, though he die, yet shall he live, and whoever lives and believes in me shall never die" (John 11:25–26). To suggest the realization of this promise, the forty-eight divisions of the cupola are adorned with white doves in upward flight, symbolizing souls freed from the earthly prison and risen to a new existence full of light and life. The designs for the fine mosaics of this church were done by Cesare Vagarini. The work itself was carried out by the firm of Monticelli, Rome, which was also responsible for the mosaic decoration in the basilicas of Tabor and Gethsemane.

Veneration of the mysteries of Bethany is ancient. Proof of this is the fact that here, more frequently than on any other single site except Nazareth, five successive churches were built in their memory, together with an elaborate monastery. The remains of three of these churches have been studied in detail. With a little imagination, we can take our bearings from the modern building and picture the extent and beauty of those which were here before.

The present main altar in the east arm of the church marks the exact site of the apse-sanctuary of the second and third churches. So, looking back towards the entrance, we are to think of a building twice the length of the modern church, starting here with a central nave and two side aisles, with sacristies on each side of the sanctuary. The width was the same as that of today's building. These overall dimensions take us well beyond the present main door, and the remains of some of the piers which supported the ancient upper structures are still to be seen in the courtyard in front of the façade.

Apparently, this church was highly decorated with plaster and paint. This was especially noted by the Russian Abbot Daniel (1106) and by others who came after him. Traces of the ornamentation have been discovered by archaeologists, particularly crosses of various shapes inscribed on the piers. These latter, in turn, most probably supported a dome, which is also mentioned by Daniel. However, the most striking feature of the decoration of all Bethany's churches was that of the floor. Parts of the mosaic designs of this second church have been recovered by scholars. They were comparatively simple in form, almost all geometrical, though pictures of fruit were evident. Three main colors were used, white, black and red, with a sprinkling of yellow and brown cubes. The floor of this church also gives some clue as to the date of the whole building. It has no crosses at all. This suggests that it was laid down after the year 427, when the Emperor Theodosius forbade the placing of crosses on pavements. The floor is also very much worn, as is indicated by the numerous repairs made to it, not only with new mosaic cubes but also with slabs of marble and even ordinary stone. Literary sources, particularly liturgical Ceremonials, refer to the Bethany church as one of the main sanctuaries of the Jerusalem area, and especially as the starting place of the traditional procession of palms on Palm Sunday (a ceremony forbidden by Caliph

Hakim in 1008, but resumed when the Crusaders came). Thus, all things considered, it is probable that the second church at Bethany was in use for a very long time, from the 5th to at least the 12th century.

The third church was identical in plan with the second and was really a variation on the former. Some of the alterations were quite notable and they provide a clue as to the period in which the work was done. The major changes took the form of strengthening certain elements of the second church: the buttressing of the north wall and the reinforcing of the piers with new masonry. The purpose of all this must have been to support a much heavier load, and the roof must have been much more elaborate. Perhaps stone was used in its construction, in contrast to the wood and tiles of previous buildings. Two domes may have been built. The masonry shows the characteristic diagonal dressing of the Crusaders and serves to fix the time of the construction fairly accurately. This, combined with literary notices, suggests that the church was in use from the middle of the 12th century onward for some two hundred and fifty years. By about 1350, however, the dome (or domes) must have fallen in, and the building thenceforward attracted little attention. As we shall see, the memories associated with it migrated partly to the eastern end of the village and partly to the west.

The second and third churches at Bethany were but a dim reflection of the most beautiful of all, the first which was built on this site. Following the close work of the archaeologists, we can now visualize something of its detail. If one stands just inside the entrance of the modern building, one is on the site of the apse-sanctuary of the first church. Thence, a single nave ran out through what is now the courtyard and into the area occupied by the neighboring mosque. Nineteen meters wide (the same as the present building), it must have been about $35\frac{1}{2}$ meters long. At the end, there was probably an open space to serve as a courtyard which was linked to the tomb of Lazarus to the west.

The most striking feature of the first church was the mosaic work on the floor. The archaeologists found that it had been damaged in places by the sinking of the bed itself, by the building of the piers for the second and third churches, and by holes made for tombs and a cistern. Still, the great mass of detail has been preserved and this makes the mosaics of Bethany one of the finest discoveries on the whole site.

The nave was decorated with a single large panel of white flowers, black leaves and black and red crosslets, all on a background of red. The over-all effect was that of a carpet divided into large diamonds throughout the field. The side aisles and the northern sacristy were similarly adorned, but in quite distinctive patterns, all rich in many colors—black, blue, yellow and red. A panel in the southern aisle was the richest and most intricate of all. Besides reminding us of the great beauty of the building, the detail of the mosaic designs helps us date its construction. From parallels with other buildings, notably the pavement of the synagogue of

148

Apamea in Syria (391), it is possible to conclude that the whole structure probably was erected in the fourth century. This is confirmed from literary sources, mainly St. Jerome's translation of Eusebius' *Onomastikon*. From changes in wording made by St. Jerome, particularly his reference to "a church which has now been erected there [Bethany]," we can infer that the first construction dates from about 375 A.D.

It is natural to wonder why were the mosaics preserved so well here. It is likely that the first church was destroyed by an earthquake quite soon after it was built. Amongst such disasters recorded in history is that of 447, which date would fit in well with archaeological information on the first Bethany church. After it collapsed, a second church was designed to take its place, but the site of this was moved farther (thirteen meters) eastward, to a slightly higher level. Thus, the rich mosaics of the floor of the first church remained buried, and therefore protected, until they were discovered and interpreted by scholars in our own time.

All of the three churches mentioned were intended, directly or indirectly, to mark the tomb where Lazarus had been buried. This lay to the west of the buildings and was always noted by visitors to the site. However, about the time when the third church was erected, the western part of the whole sanctuary seems to have assumed distinct importance, so that a separate, fourth church came into being with the tomb of Lazarus as its crypt. Archaeologists have not been able to examine the western site in detail since it is all now Moslem property. When foundations for a new minaret were being prepared in 1954, however, there were discernible traces of a church apse which must have been the central one of three. In addition, parts of the northern wall are visible in the chapel of the Greek Orthodox nearby. Literary sources stress the importance of this church during the Middle Ages. From the report left by Theodoric (1172), it is clear that the eastern church was then dedicated to Martha and Mary (or to Simon the leper), while a separate building to the west marked the actual tomb of Lazarus. Forty years later, according to another visitor, Wilbrand, there were still two churches. By 1347, however, the upper part of the church of St. Lazarus had become a mosque and soon disappeared from Christian records. Yet, the crypt was still reverenced and kept in good repair.

This subterranean shrine was made more easily accessible for Christian worship when, between 1566 and 1575, the Franciscans cut twenty-two steps down from the north side into the traditional tomb. At the bottom of these, one enters a vestibule, then goes down two more steps into a narrow passage leading to the burial chamber proper. Here, niches in the rock indicate the vaulted, shelved type of grave which was a common Jewish type. The whole design fits the terse description given by St. John (11:38): a cave with a stone laid *over* it, that is, blocking the entrance to the burial place which was lower than the vestibule floor. On this latter Jesus was standing when he delivered the majestic order, "Lazarus, come out" (John 11:43).

Continuous Christian worship at Bethany's churches cannot be fully explained without mention of the great monastery which was once attached to them. As a result of excavations, we know that it was very ample in size, covering about $62\frac{1}{2}$ meters from east to west and about 50 meters from north to south. It flanked the whole area of the Bethany churches on their south side and once had direct access to the crypt containing the tomb of Lazarus. The remains of the monastery were scattered about through the centuries, so that it is no longer possible for archaeologists to make a completely detailed reconstruction of it. However, the stonework shows that it was a typically massive Crusader building, and some of the blocks still bear the medieval masons' marks. An idea of the lavish decoration can be gained from the numerous capitals, parts of columns, and chancel posts which now lie here and there about the site. There is reason to believe that the cloister, for instance, was of very fine stonework, such as we still see at St. Catherine's in Bethlehem. Two towers were part of the defenses surrounding the abbey, and vestiges of these have been studied in detail. They were similar to so many others built by the Crusaders all over Palestine, marking the site of the Latin fortresses.

Ancient documents help us fill out the picture of the abbey. William of Tyre (1095–1184) has much to say of the foundation of the institution. Originally entrusted to the Canons of the Holy Sepulcher at the beginning of the 12th century, the monastery was greatly enlarged by Queen Millicent, whose sister, Yvette, was a member of the Benedictine community of nuns at St. Anne's, Jerusalem. Sisters from this convent took possession of the Bethany monastery in 1138, and the document of transfer to King Fulk of Anjou, husband of Queen Millicent, is still in existence. The deed was confirmed by Pope Celestine II in 1144.

The first abbess was named Mathilda, but she was later succeeded by Yvette, and this was the reason for further lavish endowments on the part of Queen Millicent. These naturally presuppose a worthy place of worship and a liturgy corresponding to the dignity of the shrine. The valuable property was surrounded by stout walls, and one tower is especially mentioned by William of Tyre.

With the fall of the Crusader kingdom, the nuns had to abandon the site. It was probably the painful task of the fourth abbess, Melisende, to lead her sisters into exile at Acre in 1187, whence they never returned. By 1347, the abbey was in ruins, though it was still marked by the formidable tower. This remained the sole vestige of the great institution until the modern work of excavation revealed in some detail the glory of its past.

Church of St. John the Baptist, Ein Karem

THE DETAILED STORY of the Christian Gospel opens on a note of joy: that of women-folk, future mothers, rejoicing. One of them, Mary of Nazareth, was a sublimely spiritual person, but she was also quite charmingly human. The annunciation in Nazareth changed her life forever but, womanlike, she promptly sought the company of a favorite cousin, Elizabeth, living to the south in the hill country of Judaea, to confirm the message of the angel and possibly to explain it a little more clearly. The meeting and its consequences are described dramatically in St. Luke's "Infancy Narrative" (Luke 1:15–2:52). Tradition has placed it in the most beautiful suburb of modern Jerusalem, Ein Karem, four miles to the west. Christians have commemorated the story by building two churches in the village, both worthy of consideration and a visit.

The church of St. John the Baptist is the one we meet first, near the entrance to the township and close to the hillside. From the Middle Ages onward, the site has been sacred to Zachary and his son, John, who was born here and later became known as "the Baptizer."

Archaeology has shown that the place had religious associations since Roman times. Statues of Venus and, probably, of Adonis were found amongst other Roman remains, including traces of a wine press and a fine collection of vases. Christians had built chapels here in the 5th or 6th centuries, one of them honoring martyrs, as an inscription shows. In the 6th century, the church on the site was destroyed by Samaritans, and all the monks serving here were massacred. The Crusaders, in turn, built an elaborate church on the spot, but it was destroyed soon after their departure. Many traces of their work remain, however, and we can say that the modern building follows the direction and plan of the 11th century church. The more recent story begins in 1621, when the Franciscans bought the site. It was not until 1674, however, that they were able to take up permanent residence and to begin restoring the church. The present building dates substantially from 1894–1900, when the main elements were restored or constructed.

The spire and dome mark the church from outside; otherwise it is largely hidden by the surrounding structures, the Franciscan Friary and the former hostel. Entry to the property is through a formal archway flanked by stone pillars and bearing, above, a statue of St. John, flanked by the coats of arms of the Holy Land and of the Franciscan Order. The interior is not very beautiful, but it is austere and functional. It is divided by six square pillars into three aisles. There are galleries above these. The dome over the central aisle, contrary to Western usage, stands outside the apse and sanctuary instead of above—an arrangement which is common in Eastern churches. The cupola is adorned with frescoes of the four evangelists and is broken by windows.

One feature which gives the building a pleasant Spanish effect is the decoration of the walls with blue tiles of Majolica ware. They also serve the practical purpose of concealing damage done to the walls by humidity during the years of Turkish occupation. The high altar (of St. Zachary) is made of different colored marbles and the reredos houses a statue of the Immaculate Virgin. The altar is flanked by colored statues of St. Zachary, St. Elizabeth, St. John and St. Anne. A fine piece of mosaic in front of the altar, admired by many pilgrims of times past, was part of the 11th-century church.

The right (south) nave leads to an altar commemorating St. Elizabeth. A picture recalls her meeting with her cousin Mary. One curious feature here is a grating on the right wall behind which is a piece of stone—a fragment of a rock, in the countryside beyond Ein Karem, on which St. John is reputed to have stood while preaching his message of penance. In 1721, part of this was removed by workmen to make lime. When the kiln exploded, the Moslems sought to appease Mar Hanna (St. John) by bringing a fragment of the rock to the church.

Four side altars stand around the walls, dedicated (clockwise) to the Nativity of Christ, St. Anthony, St. Helena and St. Joseph. The paintings are in the Spanish tradition, and they are older than the altars they adorn. Two other pictures are worth noting. Above the door of the sacristy is one of St. John in the desert, done by a member of the Murillo school. The other represents the martyrdom of St. John and is intensely dramatic. One specialist, Elias Tormo, has called it "the most beautiful painting to be found in Palestine." It was probably executed by the Spanish artist Ribalta (17th century) in imitation of Rubens or another Flemish master. Two marble statues stand near the high altar, representing St. Francis and St. Clare, done by Domenico Constantino of Palermo, in 1879.

The left (north) nave ends in a stairway leading down to the Grotto of St. John. This most likely formed an annex to the home of Zachary, as was—and still is—customary in houses in Palestine. Lamps burn continually here, giving the shrine a mystic atmosphere. The walls are adorned, for the most part, in black and white marble, though here and there the ancient original masonry shows. The entrance to the shrine is in the form of an arch, carrying the first words of Zachary's song of joy, the *Benedictus,* the climax of the Gospel story of John's birth as narrated in Luke 1:68–79. The altar is decorated with five bas-reliefs in black and white marble, showing the chief events in the life of John. Beneath it is a plaque, surrounded by rays, with the inscription (in Latin): "Here the Forerunner of the Lord was born." The picture above the altar dramatizes this, showing Mary presenting the infant John to Zachary, who writes the name of the child, while Elizabeth looks on from her bed in the background, delicately screened by a curtain.

On the floor beneath the arch is another piece of mosaic, centuries old and

corresponding to that found in the church above. However, there are ornamented floors older still, now to be found in the two chapels which have been excavated and restored. The South Chapel lies under the platform to the left (south) of the church entrance. It is a simple rectangular in form, with an apse in the east side. The total length is 13.10 meters, the width 8.30. It was divided into the three customary naves, as holes in the floor show. The most interesting feature is the mosaic floor, the piece in the sanctuary being still well preserved and showing stylized flower petals, many in the form of a cross. The structure dates from the 5th or the 6th century, but its precise name and purpose is not known. Beside the remains of the chapel are those of the oil press of Roman times, indicating the great antiquity of the site.

The other chapel lies under the entrance to the present church and is known as the Chapel of the Martyrs, from the clear Greek inscription in the mosaic floor, "Hail, Martyrs of God." It is bigger than the South Chapel (17 meters long by $12\frac{1}{2}$ wide) but the general plan is the same. To the side of the sanctuary, evidence of rooms has been found. The apse has two tombs in its floor, cut from the original rock. It is probable that they are older than the chapel which dates from Byzantine times (5th and 6th centuries). Thus, the martyrs saluted in the inscription may lie under the floor of the building itself. In any case, the mosaic tribute to them is strikingly well preserved. It is 385 centimeters long, 210 wide. A floral border surrounds it and its central motif is that of a diamond or lozenge-shaped rectangle. Ten colors are used to depict birds picking at flowers and to form geometrical figures in the rectangle. In the center of this is the inscription in Greek mentioned above. Similar pictures may have existed in the general mosaic of the chapel floor, but the modern church building makes further investigation impossible. Who exactly these martyrs were, we do not know. The names of the Holy Innocents, of monks of St. Sabas' monastery, and of three hundred Greek monks killed by Saracens, have been suggested. It is even possible that the shrine was sacred to St. Zachary (martyred in the Temple, according to para-biblical accounts) and to his son, St. John, and that the names were omitted because it was taken for granted that everyone knew them.

Walking back through the village, you can see the spring which gave the place its name, *Ein Karem* (literally, The Vineyard Spring). Its outlet is now housed in a stone archway, and above this there is a mosque and a minaret. It was this water supply which, of old, helped give the township its distinctive, fertile charm. The name Karem appears in the ancient Greek translations of the Old Testament (Joshua 15:59), and in other books of the Hebrew Bible itself (Jeremiah 6:1): *Beth-ha-Kerem*. St. Luke does not name the place directly, but his use of *oreiné* qualified by mention of Judah (Luke 1:39) means: a town in the district in the hill country around Jerusalem, belonging not to the province of Benjamin (as most of it did), but pertaining to the narrow perimeter of the province of Judah. Here, precisely, was Ein Karem situated.

Christian writers imitate the Gospel usage, referring to "The Mountain Country" and "The Hills." Perhaps it was the rich, water-nourished vegetation around the town that made further specification unnecessary, for writers of the 9th, 10th, and 11th centuries speak of it simply as "The Wooded Place" or "St. John's Woods." Even today, in tree-studded Israel, the area is outstanding for its forestation: olives, vines, fruit trees, pines and cypresses.

The name "spring" shows up first in Christian documents of the fourteenth century, and all manner of edifying legends are attached to it: Mary frequently drank of its water or carried it home; here she first met Elizabeth; here she washed little John's clothes and, for this reason, Christians wash in the spring water on the eve of St. John's feast. Thus, in time, even Moslems came to call it "The Spring of the Virgin."

From the seventeenth century onward, Ein Karem has been known simply as the town of St. John, and every reference in Christian literature carries at least an implicit reference to him. This is taken so much for granted today that modern guides have gone full circle and returned to Gospel terms, referring to the town quite regularly as "St. John's in the Mountains."

The Magnificat is written in thirty-two languages, Ein Karem.

Church of the Visitation, Ein Karem

IT IS AGAINST this beautiful, natural setting that Christian tradition places the memory of a most joyful event in the Gospels: the meeting of Mary and her cousin Elizabeth, symbolized and summed up forever in the canticle *Magnificat* (Luke 1:46–55). Antonio Barluzzi was the architect of the modern building and, of all his churches, this has the gayest and most festive atmosphere. However, skill as well as artistry was called for. As on many other biblical sites, he had not only to commemorate in fitting fashion the main mystery in view, but also to respect and incorporate the remains of churches which had stood here in times past. Thus, the building is dual: an upper church and a crypt, both now linked together in one harmonious whole.

Careful archaeological studies have revealed that this site was inhabited in very ancient times, as early as the 13th century B.C. A spring was its chief attraction and, to reach its source, a tunnel was cut back twenty-five feet into the living rock. The earliest definite remains of human buildings date from Greek times and are in the form of courses of masonry which were part of a room, this in itself having some relationship with the passage cut back towards the spring. The shape of an oil press can also be seen. That people were here in the time of the Romans is proved by the discovery of coins and pottery fragments.

In the 5th or 6th century A.D., buildings with a religious purpose were erected here. Fine, yellow stone was used, and a well was dug at the end of the grotto within the rock. Its overflow was carried in baked earthenware pipes to a cistern of generous dimensions (7.07 meters long, 5.70 wide). It is clear that the construction was on a fairly large scale. The Christian character of the building is shown by crosses scratched on the original plaster, by the remains of a liturgical inscription ("Age, eternity"), by marble fragments of a reliquary, and especially by pieces of a plate with the abbreviated wording in Greek: "Jesus Christ, Son of God. For John's and Paul's (salvation)."

Ancient writings support the evidence of the excavations. The apocryphal *Protoevangelium of James* (22:3), dating from the end of the 2nd century, tells how Elizabeth fled "into the hills" to save her child John from Herod's massacre of the children. Other early references make mention of Elizabeth's "cave," and a Western pilgrim, Theodosius (530) states definitely that the "house" of Elizabeth was placed by tradition in Ein Karem. The *Calendar of the Church of Jerusalem* lists places of pilgrimage frequented in the 7th and 8th centuries. It has this entry: "August 28. In the village of Enquarim, in the church of the worthy Elizabeth, commemoration of her." This church is most likely the Byzantine shrine, the remains of which lie under the present church of the Visitation.

Soon after their arrival, the Crusaders set about building a worthy monument on the spot. The Byzantine chapel became the crypt of a fine, upper church, the masonry being quite massive. The south wall was so thick (3.35 meters) that a staircase leading to the church above (still in use) was fashioned inside it. A fortified monastery was built around the church, and the whole construction was protected by a correspondingly strong wall. However, the formidable stonework was relieved by delicate frescoes commemorating the central mystery of the Visitation.

The upper church was 20.30 meters long and 7.80 wide, with one apse. All the south façade can still be seen, as well as four courses of the apse and part of the north wall. A design enclosing a series of small squares was engraved on the north corner, and it has been suggested that it represents the *ephod* (an apron-like vestment worn over the chest), which was in use among Jewish priests (Exodus 25:7). However, the interpretation is uncertain, there being apparently sixteen squares instead of the ritual twelve. Traces of two rooms fashioned within the very walls of the apse are another reminder of the strength of the whole structure.

With the fall of Jerusalem as the Crusader capital, this church in Ein Karem began to suffer. The Armenians held it for a time but, after they were expelled by the Moslems (between 1469 and 1483), the whole structure fell into ruin. Only the grotto was occupied by local inhabitants. In 1679, the Franciscans got possession of the site and occasionally held services there. After innumerable setbacks, they obtained permission to refashion the crypt in 1862. The rebuilding of the whole sanctuary began in 1938 but, due to the disturbances of World War II, it was not completed until 1955.

In his reconstruction of the crypt, it was Barluzzi's intention to suggest the family atmosphere of a simple dwelling, the house of Elizabeth. At the same time, he wished to preserve the feeling of ancient tradition, of memories of Christian devotion shown through the ages. Thus, while the interior was made a little more regular and the altar recess enlarged, the corridor to the ancient well was kept, as also the small niche housing a stone with a cavity in its center—said to have hidden St. John when his mother, Elizabeth, fled Herod's massacre. It is protected by a grille of wrought iron. In the north wall, two rooms were fashioned to serve as a sacristy and a small choir. The marble altar has a frontispiece in the shape of a lamb above a stylized crown of thorns, symbols of Christ's sacrifice. This, together with the tabernacle, crucifix and candlesticks, adorned with singing birds, is the work of Antonio Minghetti. A rich mosaic forms the background to the altar and shows nature—stars, animals and flowers—venerating the cross. The two figures in prayer are Elizabeth and Zachary. The floor is done in carpet-style mosaic, to emphasize the idea of close home life once more. However, the pavement of the ancient corridor leading to the well is in the form of a stream full of all kinds of fish, with the whole enclosed in a border of lotus flowers.

Façade of the Church of the Visitation, Ein Karem.

159

Most impressive are the three frescoes by Angelo della Torre, in early Renaissance style. One is of the Visitation, the meeting of the two holy women against a background of household activity in preparation for an important visitor. The second fresco represents St. John being hidden from Herod's pitiless slaughter of the Innocents. The third shows Zachary in his priestly vestments.

Crypt and church are harmoniously joined by the expedient of a ramp outside the building, which leads the visitor through olive trees, cypresses and shrubs, keeping one in close contact with nature until the upper shrine is reached. Here the theme of exuberant life is lavishly suggested by the rich decoration of the whole church: stars, animals and flowers joining in joyful praise of the Virgin. The windows themselves set the theme. They are in the form of delicate marble tracery, representing palm leaves and fruit. This was a common symbol of fertility in ancient Palestine, and thus the decorated windows themselves discreetly recall that the joy of Mary and Elizabeth was that of mothers-to-be. The altar rails and the candlesticks on the altar itself continue the palm motif. The walls, floor, and and ceiling are richly adorned with frescoes, which are undoubtedly the most striking feature of this church.

On the walls of the apse, behind the altar, Mary is pictured glorifying the Lord and surrounded by angels. In lower registers, the faithful on earth are shown worshipping at the most famous of our Marian shrines. The right (south) wall is one great mass of color, five great frescoes covering the whole area. They celebrate Mary's traditional titles of honor: Mother of God (Council of Ephesus), Dispenser of Grace (Marriage of Cana), Refuge of Sinners, Help of Christians (Battle of Lepanto), Immaculate Conception (Disputation by Duns Scotus in Paris University). All these are the work of C. Vagarini and are executed in the style of the later Italian Renaissance, but, at the same time, they are indicative of a strong, artistic, original personality: correct form varied by differing postures, set in peaceful surroundings (even on the deck of the flagship at Lepanto), all inviting to prayer, the chief object of church art. Above each picture, the meaning of the symbolism below is brought out by a smaller representation of Mary, while various womenfolk of the Old Testament, famous for their songs, are pictured in the intervals. The areas between each picture frame carry verses from Mary's own canticle, the *Magnificat,* inscribed in Latin. On the opposite side of the church, alternating with the beautiful windows, are pictures of angels by F. Manetti, after the style of Fra Angelico. The floor is one rich mosaic, showing symbols of nature in all its forms glorifying God. The roof is painted in diamonds and squares in the Tuscan manner of the 14th century. The great bronze doors are the work of Mistruzzi.

In the small courtyard in front of the church we can admire the skill of the architect in fitting the dual church into a closely circumscribed area. The four-

The Well. Lower Church of the Visitation, Ein Karem.
Overleaf: *Panorama of Ein Karem.*

storied bell tower lifts our eyes heavenward, but it also reminds us that the church could have appeared unduly high in contrast to its width. This was corrected by fashioning a colonnaded porch so as to form a base and thus to reduce the impression of height. However, the main feature, designed with the same basic motive but immensely impressive in itself, is the beautiful mosaic occupying most of the façade and representing Mary's arrival from Nazareth in Ein Karem. She is seated on a little donkey, accompanied by angels, afoot and aloft. The whole great picture was fashioned in the Vatican Mosaic Workshops according to a design by Biagio Biagetti.

Leaving the church grounds, we are reminded once more of the joyful canticle which sums up the mystery commemorated here. It is in the form of a rock wall bearing thirty-two plaques, on which the *Magnificat* is written in the chief languages of the world. The idea originated with a Franciscan, Father Aurelio Borkowski, and the whole presentation was made possible through the generosity of Catholics of Polish origin in the United States of America. Space has been left for many additional plaques.

The gates of the property are tastefully done in open iron work. Above is the Holy Land cross with bronze figures of Zachary and Elizabeth to the side. So, entering and leaving this wonderful shrine we are impelled to repeat the greeting Mary once heard from her cousin and confidante, Elizabeth, "Blessed are you among women . . . and blessed is she who believed" (Luke 1:42, 45).

The Desert of St. John

ABOUT FIVE KILOMETERS west of Ein Karem, there is a grotto where the memory of St. John's preparation for his work of prophet has remained. A small Franciscan friary has been built above it, together with an octagonal chapel surmounted by a dome. Both buildings were completed in 1923. A stairway leads down to a grotto where there is a spring, traditionally known as *Ain el-Habis,* or Spring of the Prophet. Turning west, past the basin which catches some of the water, one climbs twelve steps to the grotto of St. John, situated on the mountainside overlooking the Valley of Sorek. The cavity is 5 meters long, 3 wide, and 2 high at the northeast entrance. A rocky shelf serves as an altar, on which there is a small statue of the Precursor. Here, tradition tells us, was unfolded the early period of John's life as described by St. Luke (1:80): "And the child grew and became strong in spirit, and he was in the wilderness till the day of his manifestation to Israel."

The Western mind will immediately query whether this is the exact place where the character of St. John was formed, and, in particular, whether such a well-watered spot could be conceived of as "the wilderness." It is necessary to recall that the term is plural in Greek and really means, not "desert country" in the literal sense, but simply "uninhabited places," off the beaten track. It is quite possible that John could have chosen this spot, close enough to home but sufficiently removed for his ascetical purposes. It is certain that the memory of his presence here goes back at least to the twelfth century, for archaeological investigation has shown that a church and a small monastery dedicated to him were built on this site at that time.

Emmaus

THERE IS NO finer way to end a happy Easter day than to visit, towards evening, the shrine of Emmaus, seven miles west of Jerusalem. Emmaus is a veritable oasis in the Judaean hills of Israel. Here are beautiful pines, a sweeping view of the Western Sea, and cool, refreshing breezes even in the warm springtime. The Christian memories interwoven with this place are among the most touching in all the story of Christ's resurrection: two disillusioned disciples plodding home, their encounter with a stranger skilled in the Scriptures, their courteous, typically Eastern invitation, "Stay with us, for it is towards evening," and, finally, the opening of their eyes as he took bread, blessed it and broke (Luke 24:13–35).

The place is now marked by a large church, flanked by a Franciscan residence and college, Romanesque in style and modelled on a plan of a former Crusader shrine. It was constructed in 1901 and consecrated in 1902. The architect was a Franciscan Brother, Vendelin of Menden, helped by a confrere, Father Barnabas Meistermann, who was a prolific writer and a real guide to persons, places and items of interest in all Palestine. The church is divided into three naves by solid, Crusader-like arches, running 34 meters in length by 22 wide. The left aisle is unusual, having an independent rectangular structure of its own, a little off-center compared with the rest of the building. It has been given the name "House of Cleophas." The floor of this special section consists of geometrical designs in marble and supports a white marble altar in the form of a sarcophagus or stone coffin.

In the central nave of the church, one can see traces of the Crusader wall-columns and, at the eastern end, the three original apses. The central altar still has the ancient table. Above it are three life-sized statues in wood, showing the two disciples, Cleophas and his unnamed companion, recognizing Christ in the breaking

166

of the blessed bread. Six stained-glass windows (made in Munich) serialize the Gospel story of the first Easter evening. Over the door to the left is a picture of the meal at Emmaus, by Martinetti (1896).

In the special sanctuary over the "House of Cleophas" there is a tomb at the end of the church, facing back towards the altar. It is a reminder of one of those interesting and very human stories which sometimes evolve around the erection of a great, public monument. As the elaborate marble inscription in Latin shows, the grave is that of Marchioness Pauline Nicolay, who was born in Paris on February 16, 1811, educated at the Convent of Sacre-Coeur by St. Sophie Barat, and died in the Holy Land on June 9, 1868. She was one of those determined women in Christian history who set themselves on realizing a good work and will not be deflected from their purpose. The lady had a great devotion to the Eucharist, and her special project was to seek out and restore the "Second Cenacle," the place where Christ had "broken bread" with disciples for the second time within three days.

The present Emmaus was pointed out by a local farmer as the traditional site, and Pauline decided to restore an ancient room, still providentially standing. The cost of the property was very high (50,000 French francs in 1861), but this was no great obstacle compared with the other difficulties she encountered. The Marchioness wanted the Franciscans to take charge of the new shrine, but this idea was not at all favored by church authorities. Interminable correspondence with Rome followed, involving at one time a long argument as to whether Emmaus was really the site of the "Second Cenacle" at all. Even a Franciscan Superior of the Holy Land at the time (1866) could grow tired of the drawn-out proceedings and deliver himself of the opinion, a trifle condescending, that "women should stick to spinning, nothing else."

Deprived for a time of the active help of the Franciscans, Pauline continued the work of supervising the construction all alone, while living in a three-roomed hovel in a wholly Moslem village. This structure is still standing. In addition to her duties as clerk-of-works and paymaster, she took care of the sick in a place where hygiene and cleanliness were unknown. She also found time to do research and wrote two brochures strongly defending Emmaus as the genuine historical site of the events of Easter evening. Finally, on May 30, 1864, Rome began to turn in her favor. She was able to complete her file of documents from the Turkish authorities and, on January 4, 1867, a historical decision enabled the Franciscans to take possession of the Emmaus property and building. Pauline died in the Franciscan habit, having made profession of the Rule of the First Order in Malta in 1862, leaving forever in the Holy Land another example of a truly valiant woman. Her remains were interred in the present tomb inside the church on September 20, 1902. She is already referred to by the quite technical title, "Servant of God."

The intense faith of the Marchioness Nicolay is proof that religious devotion can remain fundamentally independent of critical problems as to time and place, for it is a fact that we still do not know for certain where Christ revealed himself to Cleophas and his friend, where "Emmaus" actually was.

The questions which arose in connection with Pauline's work have been asked over and over again in our own day and, despite close archaeological work on several sites, there is still no definite answer. Excavations at modern Emmaus were made in 1873–1875 and 1887–1890, revealing a big church with three naves and incorporating a distinctive, separate structure, slightly off-center in the northwest part. A Roman street, a typical "Broadway," came to light, together with many bottles and jars for wine and oil, marking the place as an industrial center, close to the highway through the surrounding country and a market place for the rich hinterland. During 1940–1942, the Italian Franciscans of the Holy Land, interned at Emmaus, spent a great deal of their time excavating the whole area under the guidance of Father Bagatti, a confrere and expert archaeologist. They did not touch the existing church but worked first on the remains of the Crusader castle west of the main church door. The full design of the fort was brought to light, together with further detail of the chapel it enclosed. (This was the "room" rebuilt by Marchioness Nicolay in 1862.)

More interesting still, remains of Byzantine dwellings were found within this area. Subsequent to 1943, work to the north, across the Roman road, brought to light habitations which were still older. They were definitely of the Herodian (Roman) period, as an abundance of movable objects showed: pottery, glassware and especially coins. There was no definite proof, however, that any of these buildings had been used for religious purposes. Finally, at war's end, the whole Crusader village of more than fifty structures was unearthed. One result is that we can now give a probable explanation for the Arabic name of the site: *El-Qubeibeh,* "Little Dome." The vaulted roofs of the Byzantine dwellings may have suggested, first, the plural of this form: *Qubaibat.* Later, when only the Crusader dome of the church remained amongst the ruins, the singular may have been gradually adopted as the place name.

What of the original "Emmaus," the village where Christ appeared on Easter evening? Many other localities have been suggested as the authentic site, but the choice really narrows down to two. El-Qubeibeh and modern Amwas (ancient Nicopolis). The whole debate starts with the problem of how to read the biblical text itself, Luke 24:13. The great majority of manuscripts say that the village of Christ's appearance was in the countryside *sixty* stadia from Jerusalem. Twelve witnesses (including St. Jerome) say *one hundred and sixty.* Thence the argument develops in detail, of which the following is a summary.

Modern Amwas must be considered the site. The name is clearly a corruption

Church remains at Amwas (Nicopolis).

of "Emmaus." The Gospel text is to be read 160 stadia, as many manuscripts copied in Palestine itself show. Amwas was precisely that far from Jerusalem. The disciples could have done the journey both ways in the given time, as modern Arabs can still do. Excavations, conducted especially by the French Dominicans, prove that there was a church here at least as early as the sixth century, supporting a statement left by famous Anglo-Saxon pilgrim, St. Willibald (724–726) that "the house of Cleophas has been turned into a church." There is no such evidence at El-Qubeibeh, all religious buildings there dating from Crusader times (including the so-called House of Cleophas, which has never been critically examined); moreover, the memory of Christ's appearance was never associated with that place in antiquity.

The other line of argument runs: El-Qubeibeh (modern Emmaus) was the site of the village in the country where Cleophas and his companion saw Christ. First, the biblical text is surely to be read as 60 stadia. Palestine manuscripts which changed to the higher figure are all influenced by one scholar, Origen. The longer distance could not really have been covered twice in the day by the disciples who were so disconsolate on the outward journey. Archaeology has proven that El-Qubeibeh was truly a small village in the time of Christ and there must be some long tradition behind the Crusaders' choice of the place as a sanctuary. It could have lost its true name, Emmaus, in antiquity, as in the case of other biblical sites whose old names have been rediscovered in our own time.

The majority of specialists opt for Amwas, with some notable abstentions. It seems best to leave the question open, hoping that new evidence will be found to help us situate definitely the place of Christ's second recorded appearance after his Resurrection. In the meantime, we can, with Christians such as Pauline Nicolay, cherish the memory of the story, renewing the invitation of the disciples, *Mane nobiscum, Domine,* "Lord, stay with us."

Mosaic of sixth century church, Amwas (Nicopolis).

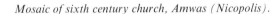

Ruins at Amwas (Nicopolis).

BETHLEHEM

THE NAME "BETHLEHEM" stirs every Christian heart throughout the world, carrying as it does overtones of the magic and mystery of Christmas. Bethlehem is still one of those few places left on earth which lives up to our hopeful imagining, for it remains simple and unspoiled. It is a town of peace, redolent of the message of peace proclaimed to men on the first Christmas night. It is kindly, in contrast, for instance, to the great, Holy City of Jerusalem: there is green instead of grey, water instead of dust, silence instead of noise. It is this theme of peace which has characterized Bethlehem's general history, in that even the most violent invaders of the Holy Land respected the town's churches. This makes a description of its main shrines fairly easy, because they are, for the most part, intact, standing substantially unchanged through the centuries.

The complicating, paradoxical factor is that this peace of Bethlehem has been disturbed by Christians themselves, with their various, separate, religious families, their distinct rites and closely guarded privileges. Regretfully, it is Bethlehem which, in the more recent past, has been the real center of such differences in all the Holy Land, the result of sincere but partisan zeal for its precious monuments and altars. Therefore, a study of its shrines is often that of a dual development, of unhappy attempts at alteration, of outright conflict. Yet, through earlier ages, Bethlehem was a great ecumenical center, and, in our own hopeful time, we must surely offer special prayers here for a return to that unity when saints of both East and West were commemorated as heroes of the one Christian family, where both Greek and Latin were written side by side in the bilingual language of a common, catholic union.

Here Jesus Christ was born. Grotto of the Nativity, Bethlehem.

The Basilica of the Nativity, Bethlehem

ON REACHING THE square in front of Bethlehem's main church, the Basilica of the Nativity, we are invited to view the church. At first sight, there seems to be nothing but blank walls—and this is very nearly true, for the façade no longer presents its original, impressive appearance. Two of its great doors have been completely sealed up, and one must enter, literally, by a hole in the wall, 1.30 meters high, which is the only aperture remaining of the third great door. It was so fashioned as to let stooping human beings in, but to keep horses out. Inside, the immediate area is that of the narthex or porch, divided into three compartments but, here again, broken only by a single wooden door.

Once inside, however, we straightaway lose this sense of meanness. Immediately in front of us is a glorious forest of columns, age-old, classical and most impressive, making this church, in the words of a modern architect, Giovanni Muzio, still "the finest in all Palestine," a veritable *aula Dei*, Assembly Hall of God. Forty-eight pillars, hewn from the white-veined rose stone of the surrounding countryside and arranged in four long rows, divide the building into five naves. The whole structure is a rectangle (53.90 meters long, the nave 46.20 meters wide, and the transept 35.82), with three apses giving variation, one at each end of the transept and a central one behind the altar. Unfortunately, the symmetry of the apses is at present obscured by walls.

The beautiful capitals of the columns are a fine example of the Corinthian style, and a Greek cross is fixed above each luxuriant bunch of acanthus leaves. The two middle rows of columns carry walls 9 meters high, and on these can be seen the beams of the roof. The higher section of these walls is pierced by windows at intervals corresponding to the bays between the pillars below.

The basilica is now the possession of the Greek Orthodox, with the Armenian Orthodox also functioning in the north apse. Therefore, the altar is almost hidden by the customary iconostasis with the usual highly decorated icons. The carved frame of this altar-screen is, as often, quite beautifully done. The many lamps add further variety, but the paint-work throughout, especially on the pulpit in the sanctuary, leaves much to be desired.

This is a reminder that what is left of the decoration of the building is but a dim reflection of the glory of the basilica in Crusader times. The building was captured intact (1099) because the population of Bethlehem came out to meet the warriors from the West and freely surrendered their town, the only example of such a thing in Crusader history. Their motive was to preserve the church from possible damage in a battle between Moslems and Christians.

The structure was so well preserved that the Crusaders were able to concentrate on rearranging some of its detail and, especially, on decorating it. Mosaic work on the inside walls provided a most striking feature, reflecting as it did an intimate knowledge of Christian sources, the Bible and early Church Councils. Over the entrance door there was a series of figures representing Christ's forerunners in the Old Testament. The parallel walls of the central nave carried the story of Christ's genealogy in the form of busts of persons mentioned in the first chapters of Matthew's and Luke's Gospels. Above these, there were more elaborate presentations of the first six General Councils. Another series opposite (on the north side) recalled the more important provincial and regional Councils.

This same consciousness of the full Catholic heritage in both East and West appeared again in the decoration of the great columns. These were adorned with the pictures of numerous saints, some known throughout the whole Church and others the favorites of individual Crusading nations: Canute and Olaf for Scandinavia, Augustine and Ambrose for Italy, James the Apostle and Vincent for Spain, Leonard for Normandy, Catald (an Irish bishop) for Southern Italy. The names were written regularly in both Greek and Latin. Some of these figures can still be faintly traced, notably those of Sts. George and Vincent. (Persons particularly interested can view a reconstruction of the series kept in the Franciscan Hostel, Casa Nova, nearby.) The transept and the choir showed scenes from the life and Passion of Christ, thus preparing the pilgrim for a visit to the spot where so many Christian mysteries had their birth, the grotto of the Nativity.

Throughout the whole scheme of ornamentation, artistry was not sought for its own sake. All was a reflection of the medieval concept that the church should be a place for instruction as well as for prayer, and "catechism" was taught by means of mosaic, painting, sculpture, and the stained glass of beautiful windows. This method of instruction in the subject of the whole Christian *oecumene,* the universal Church, in her main sources, was skilfully used in the Crusader basilica of Bethlehem.

The fabric of the church has stood for ages, due mainly to the fact that it escaped destruction at the hands of the Persians under Chosroes in 614. These invaders came rampaging through Palestine, bringing down one Christian monument after another in the most thorough work of destruction ever known there. Coming to Bethlehem, they were amazed to see a great mosaic on the wall of the basilica representing what they thought were Persian kings. In return, they respected the whole structure. Thus, the picture of the Magi adoring the Child Jesus saved the building from what would surely have been total and irreparable ruin.

So continuous is the architectural tradition that the plan of the present basilica is almost identical with that of Justinian (527–565). A former building on the site was badly damaged in 529, and Justinian had it demolished. The mosaic floor was covered with two feet of soil, and a new pavement laid at a higher level. The

174

area beyond the nave was enlarged by three apses, and the whole structure highly decorated. The Patriarch-poet of Jerusalem, Sophronius, viewed it about the year 635 and celebrated its glory in exuberant verse: the great four-fold portico, the generous apses, the forest of columns, the reflection of light on gold and mosaic, the roof done with brilliant stars rivaling the heavens themselves.

There was only one other church built on this site, and that was the original basilica of Constantine. Bishop Macarius of Jerusalem interested the emperor in building a new shrine here, and work on it began in 326. St. Helena advanced the project and actually visited the site, but she died in 329 before the building was completed. The plan of the nave is that used again later by Justinian, but, at the sanctuary end, the design was different. Here there was an octagonal structure, made distinct from the body of the church by elaborate steps, twenty-six feet wide leading up to it—something like the rotunda in Constantine's Church of the Resurrection, Jerusalem. The octagon was situated directly over the grotto of the Nativity. It is probable that an altar stood here, above the eight-sided ring of masonry in the middle of the octagon.

Within this same area of the basilica, to the northeast of the center, there was a cistern, also almost perfectly eight-sided. It may have supported the octagonal baptismal font, which is now in the south aisle of the present building. It is possible that Christians sought rebirth in the Spirit above the exact spot where Christ had been born.

Aetheria has left us a description of the rich decoration of this early basilica. She describes rich tapestries of cloth-of-gold, precious vessels, numerous lamps of various types, mosaics and rare marbles. So, from the beginning, Christians evidently thought nothing too costly for the adornment of Christ's own birthplace.

The Grotto of the Nativity

THE FOCAL POINT in the whole basilica is the spot where, according to ancient tradition, Christ was born. Two sets of steps go down from the choir to meet in front of the altar of the Nativity. The whole shrine glitters with all kinds of ornamentation, tapestries (fireproof), lamps, candlesticks and marble. Beneath the altar, in the white marble paving, there is a vermillion star of silver, 56 centimeters in diameter, with the inscription (in Latin), "Here Jesus Christ was born of the Virgin Mary. 1717." This spot is the climax for many a pilgrim who has come from the ends of the world. The date, naturally, does not refer to the great event itself. It is a somewhat melancholy reminder in this sacred place of the many disputes which have taken place around the shrine. The present star was actually

175

made in 1847, replacing the one fashioned in 1717 by the Franciscans but removed, by the Greek Orthodox and now kept in the Greek monastery of St. Sabas near Bethlehem. The date represents an assertion by the Latins of their ancient right to hold ceremonies at this altar, from which they were expelled in 1757. Attempts by the Russian Orthodox, in 1853, to force Turkey to yield full protective powers over all Orthodox Christians and over their titles and properties in the Ottoman Empire led directly to the Crimean War (1854–1856)—surely a paradoxical association with the place where Christ, the Prince of Peace, was born in Bethlehem. Still, the great event continues to be venerated in full faith, by both East and West, here.

Above the altar there is a small circular dome showing the faint traces of an ancient mosaic depicting the birth and first washing of the infant Christ. Only the words, *pax hominibus,* remain of the full lettering of the phrase *Gloria in excelsis Deo et in terra pax hominibus*. The grotto itself is an artificial cave, now measuring thirty-nine feet long and varying in width from eleven and a half to thirteen feet. To the right of this altar, two pillars and two steps down give entrance to the grotto of the Manger where the new-born Child was laid. This simple shrine is in the care of the Franciscans. The manger itself is carved from a marble plinth, which is about nine inches above the present floor level. Inside, it is seven inches deep. Opposite this altar is another, also in the charge of the Latins, dedicated to the Three Kings who came from the east, some several months after his birth, to worship the child Jesus in his grotto home.

Close archaeological investigation of the terrain beneath the present buildings fully supports the Gospel story of the Nativity. The Bethlehem area in general shows many caves in the limestone rock, and two large ones are still visible to the southeast of the hill on which the basilica stands. The original land-level (now under the church buildings) fell away into a deep gully from south to north, and in the east side of this depression there were two caves. These formed the home of the householder from whom Joseph and Mary sought hospitality, one cave being used for domestic purposes and the other as a stable for animals. It was in the latter that Christ was born.

The site was venerated quite early by Christians, but we have no topographical detail in writing until the fourth century. Aetheria has much to say of liturgical worship in Bethlehem but, tantalizingly, the page where she described how she kept the vigil of Epiphany in Bethlehem is missing. It is to another, later, permanent pilgrim in Bethlehem, St. Jerome, that we must look for interesting notes on how the place was reverenced in his time.

St. Jerome himself was probably responsible for the separation of the feast of Christmas from that of the Epiphany in Eastern observance. The two had always been intimately linked, as haunting memories in our Western liturgy still show.

Jerome brought with him from Rome the date, December 25, as Christmas Day, and on that occasion always preached for the benefit of Latin speakers. According to him, nature itself supported this dating for, from this day on, "light increases, darkness withdraws. . . . Today the Son of Justice is born to us."

Jerome also gives a description of the Bethlehem Crib: a grille protecting "what was once the cradle of our Lord and is now an altar." He makes a distinction between the two places in the shrine: that of the lodging and that of the manger. Mary bore the child in the upper grotto, then laid him in the manger placed in the smaller and lower one. Jerome bemoans the fact that, already, the Crib had been heavily adorned with silver. He wished that it were possible still to venerate the original stone, made smooth only by crude clay plaster. Thus, it is thanks to St. Jerome's acute observations and comments that we have a constant tradition in writing that the present grotto of the Nativity is the one reverenced as genuine back at least as far as Constantinian times.

Altar screen, Basilica of the Nativity, Bethlehem.

Grotto-Chapels of Bethlehem

MOST IMPRESSIVE EVIDENCE of the genuineness of the grotto of the Nativity is the presence of other grottoes nearby with their constant religious association with the mystery of Christ's birth. In the natural terrain, these formed part of the general depression sloping steeply south to north. For centuries, they remained obscure, half hidden, half chocked with debris. In 1962, the Franciscans, who hold the rights to them all, resolved to put them in order, and a gifted Sicilian confrere, Father Albert Farina, undertook the work. On September 20, 1964, the restored grottoes were opened for public worship, and they are now the most striking of the shrines in the immediate locality, second only in interest to the main grotto of the Nativity for which they provide a gradual, reverent introduction.

Twenty-three steps lead down from the Latin church of St. Catherine to the first of the subterranean shrines, the Central Grotto dedicated to Christ. The natural rock is apparent on all sides, lit discreetly by a warm, mystic light. For archaeologists, this area yielded material of great interest, proving that the site was inhabited at least as early as 700 B.C. From the religious viewpoint, however, the most intriguing find was that of numerous tombs. Here was evidence that Christians had sought a final resting place as close as possible to a highly venerated spot, the grotto of the Nativity. This was reflected long ago in the ancient Armenian legend that Sem buried the body of Eve in a grotto at Bethlehem where Christ was born centuries later, immediately above the tomb of our common mother, Eve. A simple altar, in the form of a table borne by two stylized hands raised in offering, stands beneath an arch which supports the great ceiling above. It is dedicated to Christ who realized so many ancient aspirations and prophecies, two of which from the Old Testament are spelled out: Isaiah 7:14 (Emmanuel) and Micah 5:2 (Bethlehem, of Judah). A smaller archway to the left houses a fresco of the Madonna and Child, while a third, to the right, shows a sleeping St. Joseph being warned by an angel to leave Bethlehem for Egypt. On the rocky, south wall, two pilasters frame the main altar and carry the words of the great "O" antiphons of pre-Christmas time: *O Sapientia, O Adonai, O Radix Jesse . . .*

To the left (east) of the main grotto, two others are dedicated to the Holy Innocents, the youngsters slaughtered by Herod (Matthew 2:16). The ornamentation here is quite austere, the altar consisting of two scarcely shaped stones, and the cross of unfinished pieces of olive wood. The room immediately to the right (west) of the main grotto is named for St. Eusebius of Cremona, successor to St. Jerome in the monastery he founded here. Passing through this, we enter the chamber of the tombs where St. Jerome and two of his closest followers, Sts. Paula and Eustochium, were once buried. Jerome himself fashioned these graves in the hard

178

High Altar, St. Catherine's Church, Bethlehem.

rock, but they are now empty, his own tomb being shown in the Church of St. Mary Major, Rome.

A ceramic picture on the wall shows the saint holding the Bible he loved so much, and on his grave are sculptured the words (in Latin): "This is my resting place forever. Here I will abide, for I have chosen it." The names of his chief disciples are tastefully carved on the walls, and a fresco shows Sts. Paula and Eustochium. Finally, you pass from this chapel into the Room of St. Jerome, part rock, part masonry, the habitation which saw the saint "always reading or writing" and producing, among other masterpieces, the Latin Vulgate form of the Bible, which has remained woven into the tradition of the Latin Church through fifteen hundred years.

Returning to the Central Grotto, one may go forward into the room dedicated to St. Joseph, then along a narrow corridor to the door which opens into the Grotto of the Nativity itself. Inscriptions on the walls remind us of Christ's advent and invite us to worship joyfully: "Come, let us adore the Lord. Alleluja, alleluja!"

St. Catherine's Church. Franciscan Cloisters, Bethlehem

THE FRANCISCANS OF Bethlehem, representatives of the Latin Church, having been deprived of the right to function in the great basilica of the Nativity, were forced to erect their own building for public worship and as a center for the large Latin parish of the town. This Church of St. Catherine now stands beside the basilica, and it has its own entrance to the Grotto of the Nativity.

The site is ancient, for the canons of St. Augustine built a church here in the time of the Crusades. In 1880, the present building was erected. It was refurbished once more in 1949. The Western visitor will feel at home in the graceful Romanesque structure, which is furnished simply enough in the manner of many churches in occidental countries. The arched roof is gracefully supported by a series of small columns built into the wall above the main pillars below. The organ and choir appear above the main altar, in front of which is a painting of St. Catherine of Alexandria who, according to tradition, was martyred in 307 under Emperor Maximian II. The pulpit, of Hanna (John) Rock of Jerusalem, is beautifully carved in the form of a tree, with full-leaved branches over the canopy, similar to that found in St. Peter's Church, Jaffa. On the panels in front are bas-reliefs of episodes in the infancy of Jesus. The marble baptistry, with the sculptured figure

of an angel, was done in Palermo, Italy, in 1754. The bronze doors are a recent addition (1949), bearing reliefs of the great monastic personalities associated with Bethlehem: Sts. Jerome, Paula, and Eustochium. Towards the end of the church, a stairway goes down to the newly restored grottoes beneath. Yearly, at Christmas, Latin Catholics from all the Holy Land join their Patriarch of Jerusalem in celebrating Midnight Mass here, and history was made in 1967 when the ceremony was telecast to the whole Northern Hemisphere by means of the satellite Telstar and by the Israel Broadcasting Service to the radios of the world.

North of the basilica is a beautiful medieval cloister. When St. Catherine's was built, this structure suffered somewhat, adding to the ravages of time, fire, and deliberate destruction it had experienced through the years. In 1947, the versatile and skilled architect, Antonio Barluzzi, was commissioned by the Franciscans to restore it. The main problem was to recover some of the balance lost in the building of St. Catherine's, and Barluzzi succeeded admirably. On the three sides where work was possible, he brought back to view the delicate symmetry of the original, and the quadrangle is now one of the main attractions outside the basilica itself.

Graceful, dual columns, some dating from medieval times, support Crusader arches. The most interesting detail is the capitals, twenty of the sixty-four originals having been recovered and used as models for the others. The style is medieval French, and no two are alike in decoration. Four are real gems, evidently set at one time in the walls of the basilica. Their ancient, inside section was thus quite well preserved and this is now displayed as the main feature. A large terra-cotta statue of St. Jerome reminds us that his room is close by, being connected to the restored cloister. Over the main portal, there is a graceful statue of the Immaculate Virgin. Of the whole restoration it may be said that the Holy Land Custody has added another jewel to the crown of sacred buildings with which Franciscan love of architecture has marked the Holy Land since the end of World War I.

The Monastery of St. Sabas

WHEN WE THINK of the Holy Land, we usually associate it with the personages, places and events of the Bible. It is important to remember that it is holy also by reason of people who, through the centuries, have tried to lead godly lives in accord with the austere, moral principles of the Book and have left memories of highly spiritual achievements all over this land. Monasteries were almost as numerous as churches. Thus, in our own day, we can reconstruct the way of life of ascetics of the Judaean desert, living in community at Qumran. Christians continued this tradition, as we know from the story of Carmel and of Bethlehem in St. Jerome's time. The most striking individual example, however, is that of "the Benedict of the East," the abbot, organizer, scholar, diplomat, sage, and saint: Sabas.

Born in 439 in Mutalaska, Cappadocia, he left home at eighteen and entered the monastery of Flaviana close by. He transferred to Jerusalem and the monastery of Passarion, but soon looked for a more austere way of life and, especially, for a sound monastic education under two masters of the time, Sts. Euthymius and Theoctistus. By the time he was forty-six, he had spent many years in the desert, living eventually in a grotto in the valley called Kidron, east of Bethlehem, down in the fiery region of the Dead Sea.

Sabas' fame for mature prudence and deep spirituality attracted other ascetics, and in 483 he made a church out of a neighboring cave, becoming the leader of a loosely organized community of hermits. Directed by the Patriarch of Jerusalem, he took Holy Orders and was soon abbot of all the ascetics living in the solitudes of Judaea. Besides his own community, four other *lauras* (groups of hermits) were under his direction, while six monasteries of cenobites (religious living in community), together with four hospices, were organized by him. In turn, his disciples founded three other *lauras* and two monasteries. So, he "populated the desert with a multitude of monks." Twice he was called on to represent the Palestinian Church at the imperial court of Constantinople, and each time his mission was a success.

He died in his original foundation, the Great Laura, on December 5, 532, aged ninety-four, and was buried in the precincts. His relics were subsequently taken to Venice, where they were venerated for centuries in the church of St. Antonine. In 1965, thanks to a generous ecumenical gesture on the part of Pope Paul VI, they were returned to the Holy Land. On October 25, they were flown to Jerusalem and thence transferred to their original resting place on November 12.

Today, a visit to the Great Laura takes on the nature of a pilgrimage, a real religious experience, for the spirit of St. Sabas lives on there. The rough road from the Bethlehem side descends quickly into the tortured region of the Dead Sea depression, and the monastery can be seen from afar. Like some enchanted castle, its irregular buildings follow rigidly the vertical contour of the mountainside to which they cling. The dome of the central church is the only distinctive feature.

A small door gives entry to a courtyard protected by massive walls and towers. Immediately, we see here the little square building, surmounted by an octagonal base bearing a dome, which is the main center of interest once more. Greek lettering reads: *Ho Taphos tou Hagiou Saba* (The Tomb of Saint Sabas). It is newly refurbished and enshrines the saint's body, home again at last. Pictures on the wall show various episodes of his lifetime, one with a lion in his grotto; another, his audience with the emperor in Constantinople.

Exploring the monastery is like visiting compartments of a battleship: interminable stairways, small open courtyards, corridors cut from the massive, living rock. The religious spend the greater part of the day and night in church. There is only one real meal, at midday; the menu: hard bread, olives, cheese, fruit and water. The climate is extremely harsh, and the cloister is inviolable. (Womenfolk have to view the whole establishment from a special tower outside.) The remainder of the monks' time is spent in meditation or in maintenance work and study. In fine, the way of life is little changed since the founder himself first set its high standard.

The main church is dedicated to the Annunciation and has only one nave, 30 meters long and 13 wide. It is literally crowded with crosses, icons, lamps, candlesticks and censers, reminding us of the conservative nature of the liturgy in which nothing is thrown away and all additions are made welcome. The beautifully carved woodwork of the pulpit and iconostasis is remarkable. On this latter, St. Sabas has the place of honor on the doors of the entrance to the sanctuary. There are seven other churches in the monastery, the most important being those of Sts. Nicholas and John Damascene. The first is the chapel St. Sabas himself fashioned in an excavated cave. It is especially venerated because, in a niche close by, one can see the skull of valiant monks who were martyred in the many raids and massacres the monastery has known down the centuries.

The other church is a reminder that one of the greatest churchmen of the East was once a monk here and that, in the tradition of the founder, the monastery was a center of high culture for all Palestine. The upper compartment of the chapel has a picture of St. John's death, a multitude of confreres mourning his passing. A stone sarcophagus bears the title, *Ho Taphos tou Hagiou Ioannou tou Damaskenou,* "The Tomb of Saint John of Damascus," reminding us that his remains rested here until they were transferred to Constantinople. The lower part of the chapel can be entered through a very small door and enshrines the place where he slept.

Today, the monastery which once housed one hundred and fifty monks is served by only twelve. We may hope that the return of St. Sabas' relics will help restore to the foundation the glory and fascination it once had. May it become a rich source of ferment in the Eastern Church with its traditional veneration of the Scriptures, of the universal Church Councils, of study, melody and prayer, combined with an asceticism so utterly sincere that it intrigued the imagination, mind and heart of thousands, impelling them to generous union with God. To this end, our prayer may be that of the Troparion (Collect) of December 5, Saint Sabas' feast day: "By your flowing tears, you made the desert flower. By your deep sighs, you made your hardships yield a hundred-fold. By your wonders, you made yourself a brilliant beacon for all the world. Blessed Father Sabas, pray Christ, who is God, that he would save us!"

Bibliography

THE ULTIMATE SOURCES of this book lie in the more technical studies of biblical subjects such as are published in such series as *Etudes Bibliques; Revue Biblique; International Critical Commentary; Westminster Commentaries; Zeitschrift für die neutestamentliche Wissenschaft; Bulletin of the American Schools of Oriental Research; The Catholic Biblical Quarterly,* and others.

The immediate background is a description of places, persons and events to be found in modern guide books to the Holy Land, especially that by Franciscan Father Barnabas Meistermann, *Nouveau Guide de Terre Sainte,* translated and adapted for many other tongues, especially in the form of Franciscan Father Eugene Hoade's *Guide to the Holy Land* (Jerusalem: Franciscan Press, 1962). Continual reference has been made also to Clemens Kopp, *Die heiligen Stätten der Evangelien* (Regensburg, Pustet), translated as, *The Holy Places of the Gospels* (Edinburgh-London, Nelson, 1963).

For individual topics I have consulted articles by specialists published mainly in the Italian monthly periodical *La Terra Santa* (published also in French and Spanish) by the Franciscan Custody of the Holy Land (Jerusalem, Franciscan Press). Grateful acknowledgment is made to the editors and contributors in detail hereinafter.

The biblical text cited throughout is that of *The Holy Bible,* Revised Standard Version (Toronto, New York, Edinburgh: Thomas Nelson & Sons, 1952).

pp. 11–20

Bagatti, P. Bellarmino, *Gli Scavi di Nazareth. Vol. I dalle origini al sec. XII* (Jerusalem: Franciscan Press, 1967).

Bagatti, B., "E'autentica la tradizione dell'Annunziata a Nazaret?" *La Terra Santa* 32:2 (Febbraio, 1956) 40–42.

Olivan, P. A., "Nazaret. Il Santuario dell'Incarnazione," *La Terra Santa* 30:3 (Marzo, 1954) 69–73.

Baldi, P. Donato, "Nazaret ed i suoi Santuari," *La Terra Santa* 35:8–9 (Ag.-Sett., 1959) 224–228; 35:12 (Dicem., 1959) 332–335.

Testa, P. E., "Nuove Scoperte a Nazaret, nella Grotta dell'Annunciazione," *La Terra Santa* 39:11 (Novem., 1963) 330–335.

Testa, Emmanuele, "Il Paradiso a Nazareth," *La Terra Santa* 41:9–10 (Sett.-Ott., 1965) 265–271.

Testa, Emmanuele, "Nuove Scoperte a Nazareth," *La Terra Santa* 42:11 (Novem., 1966) 308–312.

Bayer, M., "Le Vetrete nella basilica dell'Annunciazione a Nazareth," *La Terra Santa* 42:5 (Maggio, 1966) 134–136.

Bushell, G., "Nazareth's New Basilica," *The Crusader's Almanac* (Washington, D.C.) 76:1 (October, 1967) 16–19.

Baldi, Donato, "Nazaret ed i suoi Santuari," *La Terra Santa* 36:1 (Genn., 1960) 22–24.

Olivan, A., "Nazareth, Son Sanctuaire, Son Fontaine," *La Terre Sainte,* 7 (Aout-Sept., 1961) 201–206.

pp. 21–31

Caferra, A., "Oltre l'Orizzonte," *La Terra Santa* 40:7–8 (Luglio-Agosto, 1964) 223–228.

Sbrissa, O., "E forse il più geniale e felice monumento cattolico di tutto l'Oriente," *La Terra Santa* 30:10 (Ottob., 1954) 305–310.

Wilmes, G., "Cana, Santuario del Primo Miracolo," *La Terra Santa* 41:2 (Feb., 1965) 42–45.

Mancini, I., "Novità su Cana evangelica," *La Terra Santa* 42:7–8 (Luglio-Agosto, 1966) 205–210.

Olivan, A., "Il Santuario della Mediazione Materna," *La Terra Santa* 30:9 (Sett., 1954) 260–266.

pp. 33–47

Editor, "Il Santuario delle Beatitudini recentamente scoperto a Tabga," *La Terra Santa* 16:3 (Mar., 1936) 65–69.

Editor, "Il nuovo Santuario Italiano sul Monte delle Beatitudini," *La Terra Santa* 19:3 (Mar., 1939) 66–68.

Guerra, A., "Il Lago del Primato," *La Terra Santa* 41:7–8 (Luglio-Agosto, 1965) 203–209.

Andrés, P., "La Maison de St Pierre a Capharnaum," *La Terre Sainte* 1963:6 (Juin-Juillet) 168–173.

pp. 49–56

Bagatti, B., "Acri Cristiana," *La Terra Santa* 43:8–9 (Ag.-Sett., 1967) 229–234.

Governanti, G., "I Francescani in Acri dalle Crociate fino a noi," *La Terra Santa* 23:2 (Mar.-Apr., 1948) 55–68.

Bagatti, B., "Due Santuari di S. Giorgio presso Acri," *La Terra Santa* 43:2 (Feb., 1967) 46–49.

Juhasz, V., "Il Culto di San Giorgio in Palestina," *La Terra Santa,* 25:5 (Mag., 1950) 131–133.

pp. 59–70

Gabino, Fr., *El Monte Carmelo* (Roma: Tip. Poliglotta "Cuore di Maria," 1928).

Magliocco, R., "Il Monte Carmelo," *La Terra Santa* 35:3 (Mar., 1959) 88–90.

Biran, A., "Archaeological Activities 1966," *Christian News from Israel* 18:1–2 (July, 1967) 38f.: p. 6 of centerpiece illustration.

pp. 71–84

Biran, Avraham, "Archaeological Activities in Israel, 1958–1959," *Christian News from Israel* 10:1–2 (June, 1959) 25–26.

Avi-Yonah, M., "Newly-Discovered Christian Remains in the Negev," *Christian News from Israel* 10:3–4 (December, 1959) 23–25 (enclosing four pages of illustrations).

Bagatti, B., "Restauri e Scavi a Sbaita e Eboda nella Palestina Meridionale," *La Terra Santa* 36:4 (Apr., 1960) 118–122.

Biran, A., "Archaeological Activities 1965," *Christian News from Israel* 17:1 (April, 1966) 19–20.

Negev, A., "Christian Kurnub (Mampsis?)," *Christian News from Israel* 17:4 (December, 1966) 17–23 (enclosing four and a half pages of illustrations).

Biran, A., "Archaeological Activities 1966," *Christian News from Israel* 18:1–2 (July, 1967) 32–33.

pp. 87–91

Fernandez, R., "Le Puits de la Samaritaine, Sanctuaire chrétien," *La Terre Sainte* 1965: 11–12 (Nov.-Dec.) 265–267.

Bagatti, B., "Nuovi apporti archeologici sul pozzo di Giacobbe in Samaria;" Estratto dal *Studii Biblici Franciscani Liber Annuus* XVI (1965–1966).

Testa, E., "Due Frammenti di Targum sull'Incarnazione scoperti a Nazareth," *La Terra Santa* 43:4 (Apr., 1967) 99–104, with three illustrations.

pp. 93–170

Corbo, Virgilio, "Scavi al Sepolcro, Importanti elementi costantiniani ritornati alla luce," *La Terra Santa* 37:10 (Ottob., 1961) 281–285.

Corbo, Virgilio, "Gli edifici della 'Santa Anastasis'," *La Terra Santa* 38:6 (Giugno, 1962) 171–181 (with eight pages of illustrations).

Bagatti, B., "Autenticità del SS.mo Sepolcro," *La Terra Santa* 38:12 (Dicem., 1962) 299–302.

Andrés, P., "Com'era il Sepolcro di Gesù," *La Terra Santa* 39:6 (Giugno, 1963) 178–183.

Padilla, H., "Significación de la basílica y restauracion del Sto. Sepulcro," *Tierra Santa* 40:433–434 (Mar.-Abr., 1965) 6–9.

Güemes, F., "Negaciaciones para la restauración del Sto. Sepulcro," *Tierra Santa* 40:433–434 (Mar.-Abr., 1965) 10–17.

Coüasnon, P., "Obras de restauración en la basílica del Sto. Sepulcro," *Tierra Santa* 40:433–434 (Mar.-Abr., 1965) 18–25.

Lugans, G., "Presencia de las comunidades en el Sto. Sepulcro," *Tierra Santa* 40:433–434 (Mar.-Abr., 1965) 26–33.

Andrés, P., "Historia y arqueología en el Sto.

Sepulcro," *Tierra Santa* 40:433–434 (Mar.-Abr., 1965) 34–47.

Mancini, I., "Adam sous le Calvaire," *La Terre Sainte* 1965:11–12 (Nov.-Dec.) 274–278.

Costantin, G., "La Grotta sotto il Calvario," *La Terra Santa* 42:6 (Giugno, 1966) 186–188.

Barluzzi, A., "Del Modo migliore per far visitare il Santuario del Getsemani," *La Terra Santa* 24:5 (Sett.-Ott., 1949) 161–165.

Barluzzi, A., "Il Mosaico dell'Abside nel Santuario del Getsemani," *La Terra Santa* 24:4 (Luglio-Agosto, 1949) 135–140.

Corbo, Virgilio, "Gli Scavi della Grotta del Getsemani hanno confermato l'antichissima venerabile Tradizione," *La Terra Santa* 33:6 (Giugno, 1957) 167–171.

Eickler, A., "La Iglesia Luterana en Palestina," *Tierra Santa* 41:446 (Abr., 1966) 40–43.

Bagatti, B., "La Chiesa Madre del Sion," in *S. Giacomo il Minore,* Fasciculo Commemorativo del XIX Centenario della Morte (Gerusalemme: Tipografia dei PP. Francescani, 1962).

Mancini, I., "Il Monastero de S. Croce," *La Terra Santa* 41:5 (Mag., 1965) 148–153.

Wardi, Ch., "The Monastery of the Cross in Jerusalem," *Christian News from Israel* 11:1 (April, 1960) 20–25.

Wardi, Ch., "In Quest of a Tomb," *Christian News from Israel* 11:4 (Dec., 1960) 25–29.

Andrés, P., "Mort et Sepulture de la Vierge Marie," *La Terre Sainte* 1963:7 (Aout-Sept.) 200–207.

Olivan, A., "Il Tabernacolo della Gloria," *La Terra Santa* 30:12 (Dic., 1954) 357–362.

Bagatti, B., "Le Origini della Tomba della Vergine a Getsemani," *Rivista Biblica* 11 (1963) 38–52.

Galossian, I., "Sull'Oliveto. Vergini Russe in Preghiera," *La Terra Santa* 34:7–8 (Agost.-Sett., 1958) 240–242.

Saller, Sylvester, J., *Excavations at Bethany* (149–153); (Jerusalem: Franciscan Press, 1957).

Rochcau, V., "Les Pelerinages Russes au debut du siecle," *La Terre Sainte* 1967:3 (Mars) 49–58.

Barluzzi, A., "Il Nuovo Santuario della Visitazione in 'Ain Karim," *La Terra Santa* 22:4 (Luglio-Ag., 1947) 107–111.

Bagatti, B., *Il Santuario della Visitazione ad 'Ain Karim (Montana Judaeae).* Publicazione dello Studium Biblicum Franciscanum, n. 5.

Olivan, A., "Sulla Montagna di 'Ain-Karem il Santuario della Visitazione," *La Terra Santa* 30:4 (Apr., 1954) 101–106.

Donatini, B., "Nuova gemma all Visitazione," *La Terra Santa* 31:8 (Agost., 1955) 243–245.

Saller, S., *Discoveries at St. John's, 'Ein Karem* (Jerusalem: Franciscan Press, 1941–1942).

Cangioli, F., *Il Santuario e il Convento di S. Giovanni in 'Ain-Karem* (Jerusalem: Franciscan Press, 1947).

Bagatti, B., *I Monumenti di Emmaus el-Qubeibeh e dei Dintorni. Resultati degli scavi negli anni 1873, 1887–90, 1900–2, 1940–44.* Pubblicazioni dello Studium Biblicum Franciscanum, n. 4 (Jerusalem: Franciscan Press, 1947).

Olivan, A., "Emmaus, 1902," *La Terra Santa* 27:6 (Nov.-Dic., 1952), 164–166.

Emmaus. Santuario della Manifestazione in Fractione Panis, 1902–1952. Per Cura di *La Terra Santa,* Rivista Illustrata della Custodia Franciscana (Jerusalem: Franciscan Press, 1953).

pp. 171–185

Brlek, M., "Basílica Actual. Testimonio Bizantino." *Tierra Santa* 38:418 (Dic., 1963) 13–18.

Andrés, P., "La Gruta. Historia de tres siglos." *Tierra Santa* 38:418 (Dic., 1963) 6–12.

Güemes, F., "Los Cruzados: El Amor de Occidente al Niño de Belen." *Tierra Santa* 38:418 (Dic., 1963) 29–34.

Frances, J., "Los Turcos. La Estrella y la Puerta," *Tierra Santa* 38:418 (Dic., 1963) 35–40.

Lugans, G., "Grottes de Bethléem," *La Terre Sainte* 1964:12 (Dec.) 317–323.

B.B., "San Girolamo a Betlemme," *La Terra Santa* 34:10 (Ott., 1958) 292–295.

De Sandoli, Sabino, "La Decorazione Crociata della Basilica della Natività a Betlemme, simbolo d'unione," *La Terra Santa* 41:7–8 (Luglio-Agosto, 1965) 216–221.

Blondell, P., "Saint Sabas: Le Moine, L'Organisateur, le Saint," *La Terre Sainte* 1965:11–12 (Nov.-Dec.) 283–285.

"San Saba torna a Gerusalemme," *La Terra Santa* 41:12 (Dic., 1965) 344–349.

188

Index

List of Illustrations